The Palgrave Lacan Series

Jacques Lacan is one of the most important and influential thinkers of the 20th century. The reach of this influence continues to grow as we settle into the 21st century, the resonance of Lacan's thought arguably only beginning now to be properly felt, both in terms of its application to clinical matters and in its application to a range of human activities and interests. The Palgrave Lacan Series is a book series for the best new writing in the Lacanian field, giving voice to the leading writers of a new generation of Lacanian thought. The series will comprise original monographs and thematic, multi-authored collections. The books in the series will explore aspects of Lacan's theory from new perspectives and with original insights. There will be books focused on particular areas of or issues in clinical work. There will be books focused on applying Lacanian theory to areas and issues beyond the clinic, to matters of society, politics, the arts and culture. Each book, whatever its particular concern, will work to expand our understanding of Lacan's theory and its value in the 21st century.

Mohamed Tal

The End of Analysis

The Dialectics of Symbolic and Real

palgrave
macmillan

Mohamed Tal
Beirut, Lebanon

ISSN 2946-4196 ISSN 2946-420X (electronic)
The Palgrave Lacan Series
ISBN 978-3-031-29888-2 ISBN 978-3-031-29889-9 (eBook)
https://doi.org/10.1007/978-3-031-29889-9

This Palgrave Macmillan imprint is published by the registered company Springer Nature Switzerland AG.
The registered company address is: Gewerbestrasse 11, 6330 Cham, Switzerland

Foreword: Interminable

Psychoanalysis is in bad trouble. Looking back at its fate in the last century and more, one can say, in very broad strokes, that it started in a modest way, as a clinical practice, the proposal of a new way to deal with a variety of psychic ailments, available to a very limited social circle, first in Vienna, then in a handful of countries. Yet, from its beginnings in the 1890s to the moment of Freud's death in 1939 almost half a century later, it became a universal point of reference, against all odds. Its theories were controversial, but highly influential, they entered into a dialogue with a number of scientific endeavors (from medicine to humanities and social sciences), they influenced artistic practices and left a major impact on philosophy, they entailed far-reaching political consequences, they were discussed in the mass media and informed the doxa. Psychoanalysis circulated widely in the zeitgeist, from shaping common opinions to influencing the highest intellectual endeavors. Its universal impact was in sharp contrast with the relatively very limited spread of its clinical practice which was its source. This situation continued in the second half of the century, yet with a much wider spread of its practice across the globe, often at the prize of being diluted into ego-psychology, then with its role in the 'sexual revolution,' and with the highly complex ambitions of its theoretical endeavor which stood at the cutting edge of the work done in contemporary philosophy and social theory. This was largely due to the towering figure of Jacques Lacan.

There was something quite astounding about its moment of glory in the seventies, starting in the sixties and extending into the eighties. Lacan, with his seemingly impenetrable difficult style, was a very unlikely candidate for the role of the intellectual star and the figure of the new master, with the massive attendance at his seminars and his books achieving incredible circulation. His daring conceptual pursuit and innovation went uniquely hand in hand with the popular appeal. I guess the peak of the glory was the moment of the dissolution of his school (an event that I had the privilege to witness as a young student on a grant), an event that made the front-page news and galvanized the public discourse. It was a major intellectual-political event, the fate of psychoanalysis was being decided there, and the fate of psychoanalysis was then intimately linked with the state of the world at large. The big Other was at stake. Lacan's school, the school that he founded in 1964 ("alone as I have always been in relation to the psychoanalytic cause"), in opposition to the dominant psychoanalytic institutions and the prevailing ways they embodied the big Other, offered the prospect of keeping alive the subversive nature of psychoanalysis. But his institution, École Freudienne de Paris, started itself functioning as the big Other, and his last seminar, following his act of dissolving this school at the point of its seemingly highest success, was the seminar on the work of dissolution, of dissolving the glue that is the big danger looming over institutions, their pitfall. There is a French pun at hand, linking *l'école*, school, and *la colle*, the glue. The ambition was the undoing of the glue of the big Other, its ranks and insignia, its rituals of investiture. But Lacan's point at the time was not the ending, but the renewal, the renovation, the renaissance of the psychoanalytic thrust, which seems to have been stuck in the glue of his own institution. Forty years on it seems that a lot more glue was produced instead, and that the courageous attempt failed, we are facing the situation of a deep crisis.

What happened in the 40 years since Lacan's death in 1981? It seems that there is a daunting crisis looming over the contemporary fate of psychoanalysis, despite the more or less smooth running of its institutions, the continuation of its practice (although more and more diluted and hybrid), and its implementation in the academia. Its practice is increasingly overshadowed by the massive pharmacological industry that now supposedly caters for all psychic ailments, and a host of other therapies supposedly more efficient (from cognitive therapies to self-help). There is furthermore, at least in the Lacanian movement, the blaring sectarianism of the organizations fighting over his legacy, fighting each other far more harshly than their opponents. The complex psychoanalytic theories have acquired the reputation of being dated and superseded, limited to the lingo of the initiated, losing their universal impact and appeal.

Now here is a book by Mohamed Tal that presents a courageous and passionate intervention into this dismal situation. It addresses the core of the problem not by popularizing its assets or making them amenable to the common doxa and the advances in the pursuit of well-being. Quite the contrary, it proposes a rigorous conceptual research into the crucial problem of the end of analysis, for in conceiving the end the very core of psychoanalysis is at stake, its finality not only in the sense of its eventual ending but also of its aim and telos. It is a book written by an analyst, but who doesn't for a moment take his experience and practice as the sign of his entitlement, but rather as a call for the badly needed conceptual renovation which could transform its status and disrupt its inertia.

The end of analysis is, first, not to be conceived in terms of its therapeutical value, the restoration of the well-being of the subject who can then be reinserted back into the given order of things—the contention of psychoanalysis has always been that the problem doesn't lie simply with the subject and his/her symptom but at the same time puts into question that very order. Psychoanalysis is thus rather an anti-therapy. Hence, second, every analysis is always in principle also a 'training analysis,' aiming at the point where at its end the analysand can him/herself become an analyst, with the capacity to keep this experience alive and secure its continuation. This is why the question of the end of analysis stood at the core of psychoanalytic institutions and constituted the bulk of their disputes. One can say that the basic aim of psychoanalytic institutions is the transmission of its knowledge, securing the training of new analysts, and affording the guarantee of its practice. Thus, the end of the analysis was supposed to provide the entry point of legitimizing the formation of the analysts, their qualification, and their initiation, and to secure the continuation and the spread. The end of analysis should provide the passage—the pass—of the analysand to the position of the analyst, the position of authority but which is paradoxically based not on empowerment but on destitution, the acceptance of castration, the traversal of fantasy. Should one see the end as the humility of accepting one's limitations, renunciation, on the basis of which one would be able to exert the status of the analyst, an authority based on a lack? Not at all.

This is where Tal's book doesn't propose an answer that would safeguard the status of psychoanalysis but rather a series of paradoxes that undermine its secure status. The end of analysis appears rather as a fantasy, not the traversal of the fantasy but maintaining it. "Analysis may be considered as terminated when it has become interminable, when it has ended the idea of its final end." There is the fantasy that fantasy may be traversed. The end would thus coincide with repetition and provide an entry into repetition. The prospect is not that of an acceptance of castration but rather that of rescuing castration—castration appearing not as something that restricts jouissance, but coincides with it ("no jouissance is ever enjoyable, no symbolization is ever complete"). There is no ending of transference but rather the tackling of its impossibility. As for the procedure of the pass that should provide the investiture of the analyst: "The bottom line is that no pass worthy of its name has ever been a pass of the analysand who undergoes it, rather that of the analyst as such if not that of psychoanalysis altogether. What else does such a procedure declare than that psychoanalysis survives not by *transmission*—which is the case of what is instituted by science—but by *discontinuity* and *reinvention*?" Instead of transmission and securing the qualification of the analyst rather the examining of psychoanalysis itself; instead of providing the continuation and the spread rather the discontinuity calling for reinvention; instead of destitution a restitution; instead of solution a dissolution.

When Lacan proposed the dissolution of his school in January 1980, provoking a general shock which caused ripples around the globe, it seemed he was undoing the success story of his entire career, putting it into question at the peak of its reputation and influence, calling for a reinvention instead of defending the acquired status. Looking back, his act in 1980 strangely (uncannily?) coincided with what can in retrospect be seen as the advent of neoliberalism, inaugurating its subsequent triumphant march. Margaret Thatcher came to power in 1979, and Ronald Reagan was elected in 1980, both symbolically marking the beginning of another era (and one can ironically say that the era was profoundly marked by a very different kind of dissolution, the dissolution of some basic nature of the social tie). The spread of neoliberalism, in its many facets, overshadowed the last 40 years and held in check the critical theory at large, including psychoanalysis. All critical thought seems to have been powerless against this massive development and its disastrous effects, increasingly on the defensive. Is this era now coming to an end? There is a subplot to Tal's book that obliquely tackles this other kind of end. He states so at the very outset: "This book returns to the problem of the end of analysis at the end of liberalism." This is the historic vantage point from which it is written. "The joke of well-being is over," he states laconically. What's more, the book was written in Beirut, of all places, the singular place of a "disastrous success of capital, in the measure where it did realize its will to exterminate its production." The place of quite literally explosive blast and destitution. Although the book deals with what appears to be a technical problem, immanent to psychoanalysis alone, that of the end of analysis, its conceptual rigor reaches out to the question of the end that singularly defines our present state and our common fate. It continues, 40 years later, on the track of dissolution to counteract this other disastrous dissolution we are faced with.

Ljubljana, Slovenia Mladen Dolar

Acknowledgments

To those who have undergone analysis with me, I owe you two apologies: one for the failures brought to analysis and one for the failure analysis brought. I hope you find in this work sufficient consolation.

To my masters and friends, I express my deepest gratitude: Nadia Bou Ali and Mladen Dolar, who supervised this work—as a doctoral dissertation in Theoretical Psychoanalysis, Philosophy, at the University of Ljubljana—and contributed to it greatly; Alenka Zupančič and Ray Brassier, who interpreted it during its writing; Chawki Azouri, who permitted its initial question to be posed; Izidor Barši, Miran Božovič, Peter Klepec, and Frank Ruda, who accompanied its progression and critical turns; Trevor Perri, who assisted with copyediting it, first as a doctoral dissertation and then as a book; and the series editors of the Palgrave Lacan Series, Calum Neill and Derek Hook.

To the analyst of any school and kind (the *free* renegade at the head of the list), there is no possible *analysis of the analyst* if not by the analysis of, at least, also analysis itself—that is, conceptual investigation. Eluding this necessity by the lure of personal experience is the murder of psychoanalysis by its very defense. Liberalism has collapsed, neutrality is no longer an asset, and the joke of *well-being* is over. One can either be an analyst or an imbecile (i.e., one who does not know in who's service they act)—one can no longer be both.

A modified version of portions of Chap. 2 has been published in *Problemi International* (2023). And an earlier version of the first section of Chap. 4 was published in Slovene as "Nemožni transfer in kartezijanska perspektiva," trans. Samo Tomśič, *Problemi Journal* 3–4 (2022).

Praise for *The Palgrave Lacan Series*

This is an original, provocative, and most welcome book. Writing as a psychoanalyst, Tal unrepentantly calls for a high-theory renovation of Freudian praxis—as always-already Lacanian and only-just-now Cartesian. However, his exegetical acumen and incursions into philosophy serve one very concrete purpose: conceptualising the end of analysis. In the process, Tal dialectically subverts a series of orthodox clichés. For him, we enter analysis because transference does not work well enough in everyday life; neurosis is a perversion of perversion; the outcome of the analysis of neurosis thus amounts to neurosis itself (or new-rosis); the traversal of fantasy means the inevitability of fantasy; the so-called pass equals psychoanalysis's analysis of itself as reinvention in the symptom. All in all, analysis is terminable precisely insofar as it opens onto the interminable. A truly fascinating read for anyone still committed to psychoanalysis as an epistemological, ontological, and ultimately political procedure of truth.

—Lorenzo Chiesa, Senior Lecturer in Philosophy, Newcastle University, UK. Author of *Subjectivity and Otherness* and *The Not-Two*

From its inception, psychoanalysis aimed at attaining an end, its own end, the end of analysis. Thereby, it was supposed to have transformed its subject. But can one institutionalize such transformation? How does one end in the, let me say, left way? Mohamed Tal's outstanding book shows us what it is to understand the intricacies that anyone thinking through the possibility of an institution of emancipation cannot but confront.

—Frank Ruda, Professor for Modern and Contemporary Philosophy, University of Dundee, Scotland. Author of *Abolishing Freedom: A Plea for a Contemporary Use of Fatalism* and co-author of *The Dash—The Other Side of Absolute Knowing* (with Rebecca Comay)

From an author who works in both the psychoanalytic clinic and philosophy, this is an extremely forceful bringing together of the two to reopen and restage some of the fundamental concepts and moments of psychoanalysis, beginning with the concept of the end of analysis. With an amazing conceptual patience and an unyielding honesty in pursuing neglected and difficult questions, this book is a most refreshing, even if not too light, read that one enjoys more with every second of engagement with it.

—Alenka Zupančič, Author of *What Is Sex?* and *Ethics of the Real*

Contents

1

Introduction: I Don't Want to Save Love, Nor Do I Want to Get Rid of It

This book does not simply intend to add to the preexisting psychoanalytic literature on the problem of the end of analysis. It rather aims to subtract from this literature, so historical misconceptions may be corrected. It is not a thematic exploration of the question of the end of analysis but seeks to demonstrate, on the grounds of the wager that analysis can only be revived by one's willingness to bury it, that subjective destitution is coincidental to the project of Enlightenment. That is, this book intends to demonstrate that the finality of analysis is, well beyond any of the ideological figures of freedom advertised by the analytic institution, a concept of the dialectic of alienation.

The book returns to the problem of the end of analysis at the end of liberalism. Such historical endings allow us to conceive which modernity psychoanalysis had been supporting, while the logic of technicity still looks into professionalizing the practice of analysis in response to the demand of well-being by the market. Where the technician's discourse states that analysis is no longer possible as it was, this work seeks to answer what analysis was not meant to be in the first place. The question is then, "what could analysis have been?"—a formulation that suffices to introduce the great burden of *finality*.

M. Tal, *The End of Analysis*, The Palgrave Lacan Series,
https://doi.org/10.1007/978-3-031-29889-9_1

Every scission or divisive moment in the history of psychoanalysis ended up in a conflict over the notion of the finality of analysis. In fact, it can be argued that it was within the debate around finality that all scissions took place, provided that what institutional politics (called schools of thought) were there to serve in the first place was the establishment of particular finalities. Yet, what is important here—since finality is necessitated by any initiation into analysis—is the problem that (were it not for the procedure of *la passe*, or the pass) no analysis precedes its own finality. A problem that analytic traditions (i.e., orthodox, Ferenczian, and Kleinian) learned to elude by betting on experience, whether the experience they situate in the so-called *analysis of the analyst*, or in the clinical supervision and practice they derive from it. The argument defended by analytic traditions—for it founds them as traditions indeed—is that their concept of the end of analysis is the pure result of their clinical experience; which omits the fact that experience already defines itself as experience according to a finality that is imposed by a discourse. That is, I would like to suggest, when the analytic tradition claims that their concept of the end of analysis is a pure result of their "empirical" clinical experience, they overlook that what they call experience is already discourse.

Is there any novelty in stating that, as far as the psyche is concerned, there is no such thing as a clinical fact besides anxiety? What experience is there then, if not that which a discourse holds—as far as anxiety permits—in relation to its desired finality? And how are we to understand the finality of analysis accurately if every fact is a fact of discourse without submitting analysis itself, as a discourse, to analysis? This is what necessitates a resort to philosophy, because settling the matter on measurables as in any psychologizing research is religious in effect. In response to this argument about experience (i.e., the analysis of the analyst), this work argues that the analysis of the analyst is a conceptual investigation, provided that the true analysis of the analyst is the analysis of analysis itself. Any claim to the transcendence of discourse—whether as resistance or as defense—must be interpreted as the discourse it claims to transcend at its best.

The problem of finality is not only a didactic matter, however, for no analysis has ever started without intending to end. That is to say that the object of any analysis is the labor of the division of the subject. Whether one calls this division a phallus, jouissance, happiness, or even well-being now, it remains a fantasized disentanglement from structure whereby analysis is given a finality that initiates it. So when the matter is brought down to division, finality is as much a problem for the analysand as it is a burden for the analyst. We can suggest here that analysis—as the work of division—is one long debate about finality, a debate that does not end in any case, if not by the realization that the debated finality has already occurred. But which one is that among finalities? The one that, by producing a concept, frees finality as much from the discourse whereby analysis was initiated as that by which it was administered. What answers the deadlock of tradition is that analysis only becomes analysis through the failure of what discourse sustains as being its experience—that is, it is only analysis when it gets reinvented. And it is this precise failure of knowledge in a concept that, as finality of analysis, this work attempts to conceptualize; for anything else than that boils down to therapeutics.

It was in the midst of therapeutics that psychoanalysis was first established, in symptoms demanding remedies as vigorously as they refuted them, to the extent of asserting themselves no longer as the symptoms of pathology but as the symptoms of well-being. Indeed, there has never been a more efficient means of pacifying labor—the current state of things attests enough—than in well-being and the self-care that derives from it the modernity instituted by science; this is how science refurbished what makes of a person's success their very failure for their failure to become their only success. This is a point that Freud encounters neither in Hegel's works nor in Marx's but in the hysteric's passionate objection to treatment, which made him grasp the foundations of the forced choice, "either being or wellbeing," that Lacan reformulates later on as Hegelian alienation in "your freedom or your life."

Freud's formalization of division through the castration complex may have launched psychoanalysis, and it is also at formalization that most analytic undertakings have come to their end. Uncountable rites of passage have managed to revive the tradition of sacrifice under the guise of the castration complex and of psychoanalysis at large, to preach—out of the failure of science in structuring its subject—a new dark age of mourning and renunciation, a modern counterpart of the path to redemption offered by science.

This hijacking of the finality of analysis by its antagonist discourse did not go without Freud's multiple theoretical objections, among which two are exemplary. The first is the concept of the drive or the compulsion to repeat advanced in *Beyond the Pleasure Principle*, which shakes—in line with Kierkegaard—the foundations of the religious by the claim that it is not because of sin that there is redemption but for there to be redemption that there is sin. And the second is the objection to mourning and renunciation as a finality for analysis in "Analysis Terminable and Interminable," where Freud suggests that castration is not the loss of the object (wherefrom derives the aim of renunciation) but the object itself—as the negation of the pleasure principle in defense of its beyond. Those devoted trials in defense of the symptom—which are addressed in the second chapter of this book—require that we address them as no less symptomatic than what they defend; for they constitute a symptom indeed, by which Freud leaves no Freudian behind him, provided none of his direct followers did not omit the immediacy of jouissance that requires the Other's castration as mediacy.

Lacan articulates this in his return to Freud and vowed to return to what of Freud was dismissed by his followers such that psychoanalysis would survive its transformation into its own resistance. Nevertheless, for this return to end up formalizing the object as Freud indicated it (as "object *a*"), it had to be a return to Freud from the outset of what of the Enlightenment had preceded him (i.e., Hegel's concept of alienation and Kierkegaard's concept of anxiety) and at the same time a return in confrontation with structuralism's disavowal of the discursive ontology of language—the rescuing of Durkheim's and Mauss's concept of *mana* from Lévi-Strauss's reduction to a zero signifier. The return to Freud is addressed in the third chapter of this book. Lacan's long theoretical revision results in formalizing castration as the Other's lack beyond the complex, and in revealing thereupon the *dead end* of analysis—that Freud defended against the therapeutic ambitions of his followers—as the realization of the lack of the Other in subjective destitution.

The consequence of this theoretical trajectory opposes the wager of the resolution of the transference neurosis—a finality that all analytic traditions conserve eagerly as some liquidation of transference. Being a fact of discourse (as Descartes underlines in the undeceiving God), transference cannot be transcended but may be articulated beyond the inscription of the object *a* in the analyst's desire through the desire of the analyst. This affirms on the one hand that there is no other end to the analyst's desire than the desire of the analyst, and it declares on the other hand that a complete analysis is de facto discursively didactic in retrospect—that is to say, didactic regardless of whether it results in a clinical practice or not. This unfolding of the problem of transference brings in the procedure of the pass, not as an institutional modality of selecting analysts but as the necessary domain for subjective destitution to become a traversal of fantasy. This procedure is addressed in the fourth chapter of this book.

With the traversal of fantasy we arrive at the Millerian revival of liquidation and renunciation which reduces the pass to a rite, and with it Lacanism to a tradition that adds to the list of those whose quality it first vowed to interpret. The postulate that fantasy may be traversed onto jouissance is a parallel assumption to the one that sustains the argument that the discourse of the analyst may remain distinct from that of the master without its constant purification by procedure—as in the pass. This is what requires from us now not a return to Freud but to Lacan, in defense of the dialectic that founded the Freudian cause in the first place, and which, by such a traversal, would surrender to liberalism what both Freud and Lacan refused to surrender to the Church—that is, if liberalism was not actually the Church itself. For provided the true believer today is the atheist—as Slavoj Žižek claims (Žižek 2009, 101)—it is not enough to say "I don't want to save love," as Freud had earlier declared, one must also add "nor do I want to get rid of it." This is a point Lacan condenses in the concept of *les-noms-dupes-errent* to state that the one who assumes to have done away with fiction is the one who surrenders to it best.

But what is it of fantasy that may be traversed then? And how does analysis alter transference beyond the idea of liquidating it? What exactly is it for one to assume to have been an analysis? A question I pose again in this work, as devotedly as Freud did on the edge of a falling epoch, and with the same eagerness to ensure its chimeras do not outlive it.

The second chapter of the book, "A Reading of 'Analysis Terminable and Interminable,'" reconstructs Freud's argument against the theory of mourning and renunciation through his assertion of the necessity of the symptom, his reintroduction of the drive as negation, and the establishment of his antitheses to the theory of mourning as finality for analysis. The third chapter, "The 'Rescuing' of Castration," follows Lacan's revision of the concepts of castration departing from Seminar X and its reference to Kierkegaard's concept of anxiety onto the formalization of the Freudian object as object *a*. The fourth chapter, "The Procedure, from Solution to Dissolution," addresses Lacan's amendment to the concept of transference and the pass that results from it as necessary procedure, subjective destitution, and the symptomatizing that makes of it a traversal.

Allow me to end this introduction with a brief note on Beirut—where this work was thought. Beirut recently staged the fact once more that no blast is big enough to settle the artifact that leads to it or to restrict its own reduction to another artifact. Beirut is a context we'd be mistaken to consider as prior to liberal capitalism; it is rather its symptom. For the autocracy by which the Lebanese oligarchs became a republic illustrates rather accurately the grimace of liberalism where it is not constrained by fashion. Beirut is not simply a failed state; it is rather a disastrous success of capital, in the measure where it did realize its will to exterminate its production. There is no doubt this writing contains the fervent mark of Beirut, provided it derives from the torment of handling its discourse in analytic practice for a decade. But what of this mark remains essential for the problem of this work—that is finality—is Beirut's ability to ride a dream far enough for destitution to be unveiled as its only realization.

Reference

Žižek, Slavoj. 2009. *The Monstrosity of Christ: Paradox or Dialectic?* Cambridge, MA: MIT Press.

2

A Reading of "Analysis Terminable and Interminable"

The only text Freud dedicates to the question of the end of analysis is "Analysis Terminable and Interminable." This article has been subject to numerous controversies in the history of psychoanalysis, and it is a source for many theories of the ending and finality of psychoanalysis. And this is perhaps unsurprising since it contains far more questions than answers and far more debates on clinical facts than theorizations.

When one reads "Analysis Terminable and Interminable" for the first time, one might think it is driven by political intentions rather than conceptual ones. It appears that in this article Freud slaughters his most eminent disciples before his own death and writes in favor of an order that may be inherited—and indeed this is a reading that has influenced the reception of this essay for a long time. However, if one follows with precision how Freud recounts his "vertigo" in approaching the final facts offered by analysis, one discovers something completely different. It becomes evident that this essay, aside from its elegance and many lines of engagement, is a hole in the theory that Freud wants to make once and for all. It is a hole that Freud wants to preserve despite everything he had theorized, and despite everything he was left with—on the couch as much as in the theory, the drive.

M. Tal, *The End of Analysis*, The Palgrave Lacan Series,
https://doi.org/10.1007/978-3-031-29889-9_2

The essay seems to interpolate its reader by saying: "If your knowledge cannot grasp the fact, then revise your knowledge, not the fact." There is something that cannot succeed by other means than failure, Freud tells us, namely the failure of knowledge. And he leads us all the way to that. If the "alchemy of castration" leads nowhere other than castration, then the concept of castration must be revised; and if the object of desire does not cease to be lost, then the concept of the object must be revised as well. Freud leads us to approach in so many ways the central question that he debates with Ferenczi: Is it true that psychoanalysis is a process of mourning of the partial object? And if so, then does it really have a natural end that is the acceptance of castration? In other words, has there ever been a positive object before its negativizing loss for analysis to succeed as a mourning? And therefore, is castration originally a loss or a relation to the object?

Freud describes how the experience of analysis crashes at the limit of castration—which he calls a *bedrock*—and with it all its previous conceptual coordinates. On this point, Freud doesn't provide a theory, but he does provide evidence that he makes sure to deliver in the form of an ineffaceable scar or a last plea. What does Freud defend so dearly, up to the level of giving to the failure of analysis—as a cure—the status of a terminus? In this chapter, I aim to respond to this question by providing a close reading of "Analysis Terminable and Interminable." Specifically, I aim to show that what Freud indicates as a bottoming out of analysis in the castration complex is a subjective destitution. In Chap. 3, I then consider the formalizations Lacan will present in Seminar X, and the effect of those formalizations on what analysis may achieve.

The Symptom Not to Interpret

Freud sets out from a critique of the "impatient contempt" (Freud 1964, 219) with which the medical discipline has endowed psychoanalysis in its relation to the symptom, and questions Otto Rank's project, and later on Ferenczi's, aiming at the reduction of the duration of the analytical treatment. By doing so, he dismisses the performative aspirations in an analysis of a reduced length (including his own: fixing a time limit for analysis).

Moreover, Freud suggests that the symptom presents a far more critical problem; its disappearance in analysis can hardly be conceived as a permanent one. Nothing tells us, when the symptom disappears, that it will not return. So the question of the length of analysis falls back, very soon in the text, to give place to two fundamental questions: first, whether there is, regardless of how long or short analysis gets, a permanent recovery of symptoms, and, second, whether there is "such a thing as a natural end to analysis" (Freud 1964, 219). The concept of the natural end to analysis Freud refers to here is the one Ferenczi posits in *The Problem of Termination of the Analysis* in 1927, and to which we will return many times in the course of this chapter: "Analysis is not an endless process, but one which can be brought to a natural end" (Ferenczi 1982, 52).

The course of Freud's reasoning, which he dedicates to the first question (why there cannot be a permanent recovery of symptoms) to conclude very briefly on the second (in that the termination of analysis "is [rather] a practical matter" [Freud 1964, 249]), reveals to us the hypothesis he departs from: it is only if there has been a permanent recovery of symptoms that there may have been a natural end to analysis. Yet, this causal correlation of the two questions goes against the split Ferenczi introduces between them in the beginning of his text, positing that, regardless of the fate that analysis reserves to the symptom, there is a natural end to analysis that is rather on the side of character: "the dissolution of the crystalline structure of a character [that is] a recrystallization" (Ferenczi 1982, 47). In other words, if Ferenczi considers an end to analysis that is natural, it is because he dismisses the symptom: "I have already underlined with which frequency […] neurotics, who are nearly cured, remain untouched by analysis, in what concerns the symptom" (Ferenczi 1982, 47). So one may say that Freud remains loyal to the symptom—he entrusts the symptom—and at a clear distance from this notion of character. Not once does he write *character* in the text, other than to mention character analysis.[1] He is even ready to willingly sacrifice the question of the end of analysis, for that of the symptom, which he considers a more essential one: Why does it return? What function does it hold? What is *symptom* the name of? "In this field the interest of analysts seems to me to be quite wrongly directed. Instead of an enquiry into how a cure by analysis comes about (a matter which I think has been sufficiently elucidated) the question should be asked of what are the obstacles that stand in the way of such a cure" (Freud 1964, 221). This recentering of the question on the obstacles (symptom, repetition) comes right after Freud evokes that, even for those ideal cases whose "ego had not been noticeably altered" and whose "etiology of [...] disturbance had been essentially traumatic," even in such cases where one "can [...] speak of an analysis having definitively ended," "we do not know how much [their] immunity may not be due to a kind of fate which has spared [them] ordeals that are too severe" (Freud 1964, 220). What Freud means by *fate* is a chance that has prevented the return of the symptom. So Freud affirms with utmost certainty that unless a sort of chance is involved, the symptom must return (Freud 1964, 223). And he evokes right after that the drive and its "constitutional strength" (Freud 1964, 212).[2] It is left either to chance or to the drive then.

Why does Freud not add anything new about the symptom? Why this fast move onto economy and the drive? Wouldn't he have pushed his theorization of the symptom further if he wanted to? But he doesn't. He doesn't take the slightest risk in telling us anything that we might hear as a remaining step on the path of the symptom's interpretation, for he doesn't speak of a symptom to interpret. Freud approaches the symptom as one approaches a closed and consummated fact, a symptom not to interpret, a symptom that is emptied from any symbolic formation that a deciphering may dissolve.

The symptom's signification is reduced to a lack of signification. Freud doesn't only explain the emergence and return of this symptom away from signification; he also does so with the dryness of exact science. "Where there is the symptom, there is the drive," he tells us, as one would enounce the law of gravity. So what Freud starts by putting into the equation, in response to the question of the end of analysis, is the ever-returning symptom as representative of the drive. In that, Freud gives to the question of the end of analysis its first substantial amendment: "how can one conceive of the terminality of analysis in light of the interminability of the drive,[3] the symptom, and repetition?" It is from there that he wants us to depart.

Economy of the Unsynthesizable

As soon as Freud evokes the drive, he draws our attention to the idea that, against the equal division he had proposed earlier in the text between the constitutional (strength of the drive) and the accidental (traumatic alteration of the ego), it is to the constitutional that one should give primacy: "One is tempted to make the first factor—strength of instinct—responsible as well for the emergence of the second—the alteration of the ego" (Freud 1964, 212). He maintains, then, the opposition of the drive to the ego, yet an altered version of it, a version that is altered by the predominance of the drive: the ego's function is to *tame* the drive, he says, but the drive constitutes the ego, it predetermines a priori its structural failures, and triggers them a posteriori in the actuality of its return.

This division directs him in the 20 following pages toward a constant return to the economic argument (Freud 1964, 240) as a way of explaining the return of the symptom: whatever happens to the ego, during analysis or after its termination, it is constantly brought down to a differed economy of the drive, whereby a greater strength of the drive is rendered unsynthesizable for the ego. What Freud emphasizes, here, is not something that is found unsynthetized under particular circumstances. What he speaks about is not the unsynthetized but the unsynthesizable—something whose synthesis is impossible, if not by an equation that is endowed with temporality. So the entry into the economic argument that Freud proposes, and that he structures around the impossibility of the synthesis of the drive, appears to be an indication of surplus jouissance.[4] There is a surplus, an unsynthesizable surplus jouissance that the subject cannot do without and which must be regarded as the norm rather than as the exception—synthesis is the exception. Then based on this normalization of the unsynthesizable surplus, Freud advances three subsequent claims that are not without serious implications:

First, he reconsiders the autonomy of the dynamic theory and subjects it to temporality: "we should have to modify our formula and say 'the strength of the instincts at the time' instead of 'the constitutional strength of the instincts'" (Freud 1964, 224). What difference is there between these two propositions if not that this strength of drives—this surplus that has been considered as constitutional—is not only proper to the constitution of mental life, but also subject to return? What Freud tells us here is that the surplus mustn't be conceived of as a simple post hoc, a traumatic birth of the psyche (as in Rank's thesis), an original irruption of drives, but as a component that is always present somewhere in the equation and that manages to get out of hand at any point in time.

Second, Freud interrelates the temporality of the strength of drives to accidental and developmental circumstances (Freud 1964, 226). In other words, he tells us that both the traumatic and developmental factors must be conceived of as deregulations of the synthesis whereby the surplus returns, as in the moment called constitutional. He pushes the very definition of those accidental and developmental factors into the return of the drive in its unsynthesizable magnitude.

And third, Freud posits that if analysis is "a correction of [the ego's] initial process of repression [of drives]" (Freud 1964, 227), then "what analysis achieves for neurotics is nothing other than what normal people bring about for themselves" (Freud 1964, 225), which is (as in the so-called normality) a temporary solution to a temporary strength of the drive. In other words, if one approaches the drive in respect of its constancy in mental life and with regard to its unsynthesizable character, one wouldn't differentiate so much between a subject who has undergone analysis and another who hasn't needed it, Freud tells us, for they would both be managing the surplus in a temporary manner.

This last point comes in response to one of Ferenczi's claims in *The Problem of Termination of the Analysis*—namely, that an ended analysis, which is for Ferenczi an analysis that has reached its natural end, produces an identifiable subjectivity that is distinct from normal subjectivity. Ferenczi puts it in the following terms: "We can however indicate certain common traits of persons who persevered in their analysis until the end. The far clearer separation of fantasy from reality, obtained by analysis, allows them to acquire an internal freedom that is quasi unlimited, therefore, a better mastery of actions and decisions; in other words, a control that is more economical and efficient" (Ferenczi 1982, 47). Freud's position from this claim is expressed in a sharper statement further in the text:

> One has an impression that one ought not to be surprised if it should turn out in the end that the difference between a person who has not been analyzed and the behavior of a person after he has been analyzed is not so thorough-going as we aim at making it and as we expect and maintain it to be. If this is so, it would mean that analysis sometimes succeeds in eliminating the influence of an increase in instinct, but not invariably, or that the effect of analysis is limited to increasing the power of resistance of the inhibitions, so that they are equal to much greater demands than before the analysis or if no analysis had taken place. (Freud 1964, 228)

These two opposed claims, here, on whether analysis produces a subjectivity of its own or not, are not all there in opposition. One cannot dismiss that their conceptual procedures, their methodologies, are not less opposed than their contents: Ferenczi mentions a psychic economy bettered by analysis only as an aftermath of the modification of character, he mentions it as a result of something else, nearly as a surplus. Whereas Freud sets out from it to explain the results of analysis, with the strongest of his convictions in that structure—of the relation of the ego to the drive—has no without. For Freud, it is a structure that stands on economy, and which may only host a change by economy—the irreducible atom of this economy being a surplus that is unsynthesizable.

Freud moves, then, to another elucidation of this temporality of economy: if the result of analysis is a temporary solution to a temporary strength of drives, then how can analysis be prophylactic to future economic disturbances? Freud examines three possible solutions to this problem: (1) to intervene in the patient's reality to "provoke fresh sufferings in him" (Freud 1964, 223) (that he fiercely rejects), (2) to rely on transference and its frustrating factor, and (3) to "tell the patient about the possibilities of other [actually inactive] instinctual conflicts" (Freud 1964, 233). Of course, Freud points out very soon, and even since the very start of this maneuver, that those three possible methods "to stir up a conflict that is not at the time manifest" (Freud 1964, 230) cannot guarantee a prophylactic function to analysis. He is thus convinced that he has sufficiently exhausted, in response to Ferenczi's claim, all clinical possibilities of ensuring a permanent resolution of repetition.

So, for Freud, any possible result of analysis should be conceived of in terms of an enhanced economy within the same structure—that is for him the relation of the ego to the drive (which certainly doesn't go without saying that when Freud speaks of the ego, throughout this article, he mostly speaks of the subject of the unconscious[5]). While for Ferenczi, he speaks of a dissolution of structure whereby a new structure is achieved (a recrystallization)—a structure that Ferenczi sustains under the term "character," and which doesn't feature the same duality present in Freud's. In this respect, the whole debate leads to two different concepts of subjectivity. What is subjectivity for Freud, and what is it for Ferenczi? Why does it allow changeability of structure for Ferenczi, and why does it not for Freud? This is what we will try to address next, in order to grasp Freud's following move in the article. For if the debate that takes place before us may have appeared as a clinical one, the quarrel about whether analysis permits a changeability in structure shows us that it was a conceptual debate all along. The kernel of Freud's disagreement with Ferenczi, as we will see, pertains to the question of subjectivity, and thus relates to the status given to the structure of the unconscious.

The Quarrel About Subjectivity

Ferenczi doesn't offer a recollection of his findings in a renewed introduction of what he considers to be the psychic apparatus. What he leaves us with are clinical notes, remarks, and fragments of theories that require a synthesis. To understand Ferenczi's position from the question of subject and structure, we shall set out from the observation that he had started to take a noticeably different theoretical path from Freud's since the days of *Beyond the Pleasure Principle* (1920), more precisely since Freud's conceptualization of the death drive.

As underlined by José Jiménez Avello, Ferenczi disagrees with Freud's attribution of the death drive to the order of the congenital or the constitutional, since for him it is impossible that the drive had been a death drive since the beginning of psychic life, and there must have been a traumatic element to direct it onto such a functioning (Avello 2000, 32). Ferenczi articulates this traumatic element through a substantial work on the process of mimicry or primary identification that he posits to be prior and causal to object relations in psychic development. Ferenczi tells us that what takes place in the infant's mimicry is an introjection of "alien transplants" that are "psychical contents" pertaining to the adult's desire, which the infant's psyche will host, henceforth, as if they were its own, implicating therefore feelings of displeasure (Ferenczi 1985, 134–203).

The subject will respond to those "un-pleasurable alien transplants," experienced as the traumatic intrusion of the other, by *passional* reactions, says Ferenczi, similar to what Freud describes by the death drive (Avello 2000). Avello interprets here Ferenczi's use of *passion* from the outset of his reference to Descartes in the postscriptum of *Confusion of Tongues*: passion for Ferenczi, and along the Cartesian line of thought, is the subject's response—by suffering—to their own transformation in consequence of their environment, that is to say the Other (Avello 2000).

Avello concludes his article on a pivotal interpretation that may shed light on the crux of the quarrel between Freud and Ferenczi: Ferenczi opposes particularly Freud's attribution of a masochistic quality to the death drive, for in doing so he would be legitimizing the oppressive action of the Other on the subject by his theory of the psychic apparatus (Avello 2000). In that, Freud's classification of the death drive in the constitutional order reflects, for Ferenczi, Freud's willingness to renounce the "essence" (as interpreted by Avello) of the subject for the other's oppression. In other words, Freud theorizes the subject, in their psychic apparatus, as already oppressed, that is to say he theorizes the subject as already occluding the Other.

If we turn to Wladimir Granoff's introduction of Ferenczi's concepts into French psychoanalytic culture in the 1950s, we would notice that he didn't shy away from this cause. If Avello shows us the other's oppression in Ferenczi's works on mimicry and primary identification (i.e., the imaginary[6] other's oppression of the subject), Granoff underlines this same oppressive process in the subject's entry into the symbolic. *Thalassa*, Granoff tells us, is a term by which Ferenczi introduces to us "the signifier as such," the signifier as a *pure body* deprived from its symbolic dimension—that is to say the status of the symbol before the subject's inscription in the symbolic (Granoff 1958, 89).

Then Granoff draws our attention back, as Avello does, to Ferenczi's refusal to conceive psychic development within the limits of Freud's reliance on ontogenesis. The access to the symbolic, and thereby to genital sexuality, Ferenczi tells us, is a "phylogenic catastrophe" that exceeds the "ontogenic" one (Ferenczi 1938, 51). The term *phylogenic* Ferenczi employs, here, does not only stress that the access to genital sexuality is in correlation to the access to the phallic key but also that the constitution of language in the child's psyche is a genetic process of its own, and the entry into the symbolic is to be approached not as an ontogenesis. Granoff continues, then, returning to Ferenczi's letter to Freud in 1912, where he had written about a certain duality in the status of the symbol: the symbol up until then had been approached only from the outset of the order it establishes (the symbolic), but it has another dimension one can grasp if one approaches it from without. In Granoff's words (that I translate from French): "[Ferenczi] makes this remark that is fundamental to him that the symbol is to envisage before and after repression. He introduces two neologisms: phenero-symbolism and crypto-symbolism. To judge the example that is given, one finds in it the apprehension of the effects called by Lacan, Metaphoric and Metonymic" (Granoff 1958, 92). Let us retain from Granoff's disquisition of Ferenczi's line of thought the idea that the status of the symbol is transformed by repression. What the symbol is before repression is a phenomenon, a body, or a form; and what it becomes after repression is a crypt—that is, as in *crypta*, a cemetery under a language. In short, Ferenczi grasps very early the mortification involved in the establishment of the symbol which, for him, is not only the burial of the thing as such, but the subject's as well—he establishes already a line that leads to Lacan's *aphanisis*.

Miguel Gutiérrez-Peláez formalizes the argument initiated by Granoff, through a reinterpretation of Ferenczi's position from the symbolic, from the outset of Lacan's concept of *lalangue*: "What if there is an original (failed) rejection [...] of the symbolic order in the infant? What if language itself constitutes the Urtrauma" (Gutiérrez-Peláez 2015, 6)? For Gutiérrez-Peláez, this is how Ferenczi redirects Freud's question. Then he continues: "Ferenczi intends to unveil a realm prior to language, free of trauma; concepts such as 'Thálassa' (1924), the primordial sea, or 'infant,' he who is speechless or unable to speak, point directly to this"

(Gutiérrez-Peláez 2015, 6). From this, Gutiérrez-Peláez articulates this state prior to repression or trauma to desire in Ferenczi's writings: desire is, for Ferenczi, the desire to return to this primordial state, and analysis must operate in the direction of this desire (Gutiérrez-Peláez 2015, 7).

Nevertheless, following Ferenczi's progression to this undivided—primordial, nondetermined, unoppressed, semidissolved—"essence" of the subject, leads us to no simple conclusion. We are left with a far more complex conceptual problem, which, as Gutiérrez-Peláez points out, Ferenczi wasn't unaware of: If the subject's inscription in the symbolic is traumatic, what is then their non-inscription in it (Gutiérrez-Peláez 2015, 12)? Is it not equally traumatic? Is not the subject's capture by their jouissance with no Other to refrain it, or to "oppress" it as Ferenczi says, even more traumatic than one's oppression by the Other? Is there such a thing as this without or opposite side of trauma in the psychic apparatus, which Ferenczi seems to want analysis to reach, like a process of "healing" (Gutiérrez-Peláez 2015, 16)? It is perhaps with this transcending direction to analysis implied by the idea of the primordial essence that Freud engages in his response when he tells us that changeability in structure is but an economic one, and thereby a temporary one. For Freud, the structure of the psychic apparatus must include this oppressive Other, it must function as a dialectic that has neither a state that is prior to it, nor a without. Although Freud will allude to the unsplit subject of drives later in the text, he will do so to reinscribe it in the dialectic of alienation. Freud doesn't believe that there is a point that precedes the dialectic that one must reach; transcendence for him is but a lure. This is the idea that he sustains since the beginning of the article by the necessity of the symptom and the dichotomy of ego and drive, then in the idea of the unsynthesizable surplus, and later in his defense of his concept of the duality of the drive.

The crux of the debate between Freud and Ferenczi, when it comes to the concept of structure, may be summarized in the following: Ferenczi posits that there is an unsplit primordial subjectivity governed by the life drive whose oppression (by the introjection of the Other) produces the traumatic splitting and the appearance of the death drive. Freud, on the other hand, doesn't only disagree with Ferenczi on the concept of the death drive that he considers to be there since the beginning of psychic life. The following section will show that he even disagrees with Ferenczi on the concept of the life drive and with regard to the object of the drive. Freud will show us that the life drive isn't a search for a primary experience of pleasure, as Ferenczi posits, nor does it have a positive object. The drive, for Freud, doesn't settle for pleasure; it wants what is beyond pleasure that is jouissance, and it is this negation of pleasure that is involved in the drive that requires an object whose positivization is never enough.

The Drive as Negation

Ferenczi posits that there is an end to repetition that may be reached when one accesses their primordial essence. And this is what Freud argues against in his essay. In *The Problem of Termination of the Analysis*, and right before mentioning the necessity of the "dissolution of the crystalline structure of character" for analysis to naturally end, Ferenczi writes: "Originally, for the child, all that has a good taste is good. He has therefore to learn to consider and feel that numerous things that have a good taste are bad, and to discover that obedience to precepts implicating difficult renunciations transforms into a source of felicity and of extreme satisfaction. […] Every renunciation of the drive and every affirmation of unpleasure are still, clearly, linked to the sentiment of non-truth, that is to say of hypocrisy" (Ferenczi 1982, 46).

So Ferenczi tells us that knowledge—the ego-ideal—involves nontruth and consequently unpleasure in how it affects the drive, an argument Freud will go along with for a start: Freud begins his response by a revision of the ego's status, reminding us that the ego's establishment operates an inversion of the subject of drives from an inside to an outside of the ego,[7] therefore that the ego is not the true self, that it represents the true self only by subtracting it (Freud 1964, 235).

But then, Freud turns back to address Ferenczi's very concept of truth—the drive—on the basis of which he constructs his nontruth. What is this truth Ferenczi articulates to the drive, and whose loss occurs by "obedience" and "renunciation"? Ferenczi writes: "Originally, for the child, all that has a good taste is good. […] Every renunciation of the drive and every affirmation of unpleasure are still, clearly, linked to the sentiment of non-truth" (Ferenczi 1982, 46). Is it not the "primary experience of pleasure" that Ferenczi tells us to be the subject of this "renunciation of the drive"? And does it not suppose, already, that what the drive is after is pleasure? Furthermore, if Ferenczi conceives the drive as this "strong tendency" (as he calls it) to access primary experiences of pleasure, does he not suppose, as well, that this drive has an original object, and thereby that its object is originally a positive one? This drive, seeking pleasure in a positive object, is conceptually sufficient for him to throw the whole of the problem of enjoyment on the Other's back, and endow this Other, by the same token, with as much positivity as that of the object he makes him restrict. This Other becomes positive enough, when one departs from the drive as a search for pleasure in the partial object, for truth to expulse him, now, to reach its original pleasures. In fact, Ferenczi's construction of the idea of truth—of enjoyment—bypasses the concepts of surplus and negation from beginning to end, and it is precisely there where Freud directs our attention in his response.

First, Freud tells us that "obedience" (to use Ferenczi's words)—which he translates into "repression"—is not the renunciation to an original pleasure but to a negation that he likens to Flavius Josephus's offense to the Christendom (Freud 1964, 236). What is it that one represses? Not a pleasure but a questioning of belief, Freud tells us, that aims at the symbolic as such (the Christendom), and which this symbolic has, then, to erase and substitute in the progression of its script (Freud 1964, 236). "Jesus, son of Damneus," Josephus tells us, obtained his priesthood by Albinus, in response to Ananus's assembling of a Sanhedrim of judges without his consent; after Ananus had condemned "the brother of Jesus, who was called Christ" (Josephus n.d.) to be stoned for breaking the law. What is Josephus's narrative other than a negation of that Jesus is Christ and son of God? Does he not tell us that God is, after all, a split subject whose chance has led to a divineness that is strange to him? Freud tells us that repression is the result of a drive to negate, not of a drive to an original pleasure. What is repressed is a negation, and a negation of the sufficiency of the symbolic—which is a negation of satisfaction by the pleasure principle as we will see later on.

Second, Freud reunifies the drive and the ego which he had kept extrapolated since the beginning of the text: "id and ego are originally one," he says and then adds that the drive lays the foundations of the ego, which shares its "lines of development, trends, and reactions" (Freud 1964, 240). So what Freud advances here is that there is an "ego" that is a realization of the drive as much as there is one that synthetizes it, that there is an "ego" that acts in the service of the drive as much as there is one that acts against it: "With the recognition that the properties of the ego which we meet with in the form of resistances can equally well be determined by heredity [its heredity in relation to the drive] as acquired in defensive struggles, the topographical distinction between what is ego and what is id loses much of its value for our investigation" (Freud 1964, 241).

Why would Freud stress this indistinction of the ego and the id at the meeting point of resistance? He claims, in fact, that resistance sustains a subject that is unsplit, a subject whose splitting by the signifier is aborted through resistance; and advances that this unsplit subject of drives—this ego who acts, by resistance, in the service of drives—is ungraspable enough (by the signifier), to render our "topographical distinction between what is ego and what is id lose much of its value." Therefore, if it is only by resistance that this subject of drives may formulate itself, can one really name it a resistance?

This brings us to the third point where Freud revises this naming. He had mistakenly called them, he says, the "resistances from the Id" (in *Inhibitions, Symptoms and Anxiety*) and decides to attribute them, now, to "the behavior of the two primal instincts, their distribution, mingling and diffusion" (Freud 1964, 242). What Freud considered to be the resistance from the id, he tells us, is the drive's method of "defending itself" against recovery, a method by which it shows itself to be "absolutely resolved to hold on to illness and suffering" (Freud 1964, 242). The subject of drives needs to suffer, he tells us, it needs pleasure to fail in order for it to subsist. For "resistance," in fact, has always been in a direct correlation to subsistence; before that got sacrificed for an idea of truth in the subject of the unconscious. Was it not such reputable necessity to resist, to risk one's life for one's freedom? Freud points us to that the widespread denigration of resistance, among psychoanalysts, stemmed from their belief in the Other's knowledge? It appears that Freud changed the position he maintained in *Inhibitions, Symptoms and Anxiety*; he argues now, as in Flavius Josephus's defense he quotes, that resistance is self-defense and thereby subsistence. Furthermore, he tells us if there is a self, an unsplit self, it is that which resists, and resists by suffering (jouissance); and not that which seeks pleasure as Ferenczi posits, but the failure of pleasure, the negation of pleasure, in that it must be conceived of as being primordially masochistic.

Fourth, Freud proceeds to explain that this masochism of the drive is the kernel of psychic normality, as opposed to the thesis sustained by Ferenczi (as by himself prior to the death drive) claiming "that mental events are exclusively governed by the desire for pleasure" and that this masochism is an abnormality that analysis must abolish (Freud 1964, 243). "These phenomena are unmistakable indications of the presence of a power in mental life which we call the instinct of aggression or of destruction according to its aims, and which we trace back to the original death instinct of living matter. It is not a question of an antithesis between an optimistic and a pessimistic theory of life. Only by the concurrent or mutually opposing action of the two primal instincts—Eros and the death-instinct—, never by one or the other alone, can we explain the rich multiplicity or the phenomena of life" (Freud 1964, 243).

There is a radical conceptual necessity, Freud argues, and not just a "pessimistic theory of life," giving place to this masochism within our conception of our very psychic normality. If we do not meet this necessity with a dualistic theory of drives, the drive will remain an instinct, and "the rich multiplicity or the phenomena of [human] life" will remain unexplained. He even warns us against rushing into optimistic conclusions in dealing with this masochism—that is to say rushing into submitting it to our belief. Freud tells us to simply "bow to the superiority of the forces against which we see our efforts come to nothing" (Freud 1964, 243). Bow to the necessity of jouissance, he tells us, there can be no subjectivity without it.

Fifth, Freud addresses the inherent duality of the drives, using the example of homosexuality, where heterosexual and homosexual tendencies "are in a state of irreconcilable conflict" (Freud 1964, 244). He asks why the two opponents don't "divide up the available quota of libido between them according to their relative strength, since they are able to do so in a number of cases" (Freud 1964, 244). In other words, why doesn't this duality resolve itself, why does it subsist as a conflict of a constant stance? Why does it remain a constant force between two? Why does it not become one? Freud tells us, "We are forced to the conclusion that the tendency to a conflict is something special, something which is newly added to the situation, irrespective of the quantity of libido" (Freud 1964, 244). What conclusion does he say he is forced to? Is it not that there is a final cause that exceeds the material one—irrespective of the quantity of libido—which, had things been left to it, would have consumed this duality and produced a unity instead? In fact, if Freud called his advancement of the dualistic theory (of drives in *Beyond the Pleasure Principle*) the third step in the theory of drives, then he might be introducing a fourth one through Empedocles's supplement and prepared here by this negation of the material cause. For in his third step, Freud proposes that if the drive's trajectory leads back by the pleasure principle to the inanimate it departs from (the complete discharge), then the drive is basically a death drive; while he posits the life drive's function to be a postponing or suspension of this complete discharge whereby a sustainment of life takes place. This is the requirement of a beyond the pleasure principle for life to be sustained (by an accumulation of excitation without discharge), for the pleasure principle can only lead back to death. And it is in response to this deadlock—of accumulated excitation—that Freud advances the nirvana principle as an antidote that is operated through the death drive's short-circuiting of the life drive. Nevertheless, although the opposition of the life drive to the death drive was already drawn for us in the third step, the two opponents were still posited to be in a constant battle with each other, giving to the quantitative factor an exclusivity in explaining which of them was to prevail. In what Freud tells us here, however, these two opponents, as Empedocles's love and strife will show, are in a constant succession of ruling. This cyclical succession in ruling between the life drive and the death drive underlines that they are rather two successive and opposite operations than opponents, two successive logical times and opposite positions of the relation to lack (of being), that always leads back to its beginning.

I begin by reading Lacan's formalization of this fourth step in Seminar XI—which he interestingly does without a reference to Freud's use of Empedocles—in order to grasp retroactively Empedocles's supplement that Freud introduces. Lacan sets out from the same question of the constancy of tension, which Freud uses to introduce the question of the inherence of duality of drives (in "Analysis Terminable and Interminable"). He departs from the idea that if Freud qualifies the drive as a constant force, then it cannot be a biological function, for if it were it would have been regulated by cycles of excitation and discharge. He consequently positions the drive and the biological function, in a rapport of "antinomy." That is, what the drive properly operates, as opposed to the instinct, is a negation of satisfaction. So, the drive, Lacan tells us, "rectifies" satisfaction—which is operated through the pleasure principle—by confronting it to its "impossibility" (Lacan 1981, 165–66). This impossibility of satisfaction is the desexualizing effect of the drive, which is the consequence of the fact that the drive's object—contrarily to the object of need—is a negativity (Lacan 1981, 167). In other words, the drive's object is the negation of the object of need—it is the surplus that exceeds it. The drive, Lacan tells us, is "indifferent" to its object. It isn't interested in what its object is as much as it is interested in sustaining that it exists. And given that the object is not the finality of the drive, the drive's course isn't directed onto the object, but rather around it, "la pulsion en fait le tour" (Lacan 1981, 168). What is the finality of the drive then? What does the drive operate through in its circulation around the object?

To respond to this question, Lacan returns, first, to the source of the drive, the erogenous zones. The erogenous zone is an opening in the body (mouth, anus, genitals, eyes, ears) that mediates its relation to its exteriority. Yet this mediation of the erogenous zone exceeds the self-preserving biological finality—of excrement for the anal zone for example—that is of the order of need; it exceeds it in that it constitutes a rapport between two heterogeneous domains: organic sexuality (i.e., determined by the organism's need of reproduction) from one side, and the Other and its demand (i.e., the law of language and the signifier) from the other side. And this mediation, in the strict sense of the word, is impossible to produce by anything else than a "montage," a montage of the organic with the symbolic. This montage is the drive in its departure from the organic to the symbolic through the erogenous zone, which Lacan comically induces to us earlier in the following comment (Lacan 1981, 169): "For the moment, I am not fucking, I am talking to you. Well! I can have exactly the same satisfaction as if I were fucking. That's what it means. Indeed, it raises the question of whether in fact I am not fucking at this moment" (Lacan 1981, 166).

Why is this montage of *fucking* by *talking* a necessity? Why can't we leave the organic to operate by itself, as it does in all other animal species? For the organic operation onto the satisfaction of need, the satisfaction of need—as organic need of reproduction—is in itself a subjective death for the preservation of the organism, if not that of the species. And this is a point introduced since Darwin and abundantly used by Freud in *Beyond the Pleasure Principle*. So the drive, in its montage of the organic with the symbolic, is already a negation of this death by satisfaction, and thus a death negating life drive. On those bases—that the drive mustn't reach organic satisfaction, and thereby death—Lacan poses for us the partiality of the drive (Lacan 1981, 176–77): "That sexuality is realized only through the operation of the drives in so far as they are partial drives, partial with regard to the biological finality of sexuality." In other words, the drive is fundamentally partial to guarantee that satisfaction—as "biological finality of sexuality"—is only met partially. Then, putting this necessity of bypassing death in satisfaction as primary condition, Lacan operates a reversal of the status of the erogenous zone, from a source of the drive as montage, to an *appareil*, or tool, of the montage as a necessity. So he tells us that it is because of the necessity of the drive—in sustaining life by montage—that the openings of the body are rendered erogenous, and not the reverse. In other words, the drive becomes the essential source of its substantial source (Lacan 1981, 177).

From this, Lacan addresses the other half of the drive's circular trajectory around the object—namely, its return to the erogenous zone: "What is fundamental at the level of each drive is the movement outwards and back in which it is structured" (Lacan 1981, 177). In fact, it is in its return—not in its departure—that he identifies the drive's realization; the drive returns, he tells us, as if it were the Other's—that is to say it returns as precluded in the montage it had departed to operate. In this return, Lacan continues, the drive would have attained "its satisfaction [that is rendering the organic satisfaction impossible by mounting it to the symbolic, barring it by the object as void] without attaining its aim," which remains this organic satisfaction. Thus, "the [true] aim [of the drive] is the way taken," which is the circular course that guarantees its "return into circuit"—the circuit of the constant force in the erogenous zone, that is a bypassing or an off-circuit of the biological function of reproduction (Lacan 1981, 178–79).

Now this aimless drive—whose satisfaction is in constant failure in reaching satisfaction, whose object it wants to always miss, and whose essence is to sustain nothing more than a constant force or a tension by a circuit—Lacan tells us, is "the mode of the headless subject, for everything is articulated in it in terms of tension, and has no relation to the subject other than one of topological community" (Lacan 1981, 181). Here we must be reminded that the subject tout-court, the *headed* subject let's say, is the one appointed by the Other and represented—that is to say effaced—by the signifier. The headed subject is the split subject of desire that is alienated from the Other in consequence of signification—the "sujet troué" (Lacan 1981, 184). Therefore, what Lacan names by the *headless subject* is, in fact, a negation of the split subject which, however, doesn't lead to an absence of subjectivity but to an unsubjected subjectivity. In other words, the headless subject is a subjectivation that cannot be grasped, one that remains uncaught by signification and that is only witnessed as a trace that has no meaning (seen or heard, but not grasped), "a subjectification without subject, a bone, a structure, an outline, which represents one side of the topology" (Lacan 1981, 184). It is in this sense that the headless subject, Lacan tells us, is solely "articulated in terms of tension." This interplay between the split subject and the headless subject constitutes already the groundwork for the theory of alienation and separation Lacan is moving toward in this introduction.

To show us this headless subject as ungraspable trace, Lacan relies on the eye: he tells us—in his revision of the dialectic of the Sartrean gaze—that it is by the very introduction of the other and his gaze, that the subject seen seeing, through the keyhole, is seen seeing the object; if it weren't for this other seeing him, he would have still been "trying to see [...] the object as absence"—that is the lack of it (Lacan 1981, 182). Shame, as Sartre tells us, but first the object whose correlative is shame, as Lacan adds, are both consequent to the other's gaze. So, it requires the other, seeing, for (the image of) the object to exist as seen by the subject. This seeing of the other is the drive's "return form, which is the true active drive"—that is to say the moment where the drive's action on the subject—which is *pain*—is manifested as inflicted by the other (Lacan 1981, 182): "It is, he [Freud] tells us, at the moment when the loop is closed, when it is from one pole to the other that there has been a reversal, when the other has come into play, when the subject has taken himself as the end, the terminus of the drive. At this moment, pain comes into play in so far as the subject experiences it from the other" (Lacan 1981, 183).

This pain the drive returns with, then, is the jouissance that the subject extracts from the Other—and which, if it weren't to the return of the drive, would have remained inscribed in the Other, and with it the subject as we have seen previously (Lacan 1981, 183). "What is at issue in the drive is finally revealed here—the course of the drive is the only form of transgression that is permitted to the subject in relation to the pleasure principle" (Lacan 1981, 183).

To summarize the three statuses of the subject, and the two movements occurring between them, that this transgression of the pleasure principle works through, we may say the following: (1) there is the transgression of the biological function of reproduction whereby the reach to pleasure in discharge implicates that the subject is already dead, that it is a nonsubjectivity. This first transgression is allowed by the montage whose result is the headed subject or the split subject that is appointed by the Other, and thereby dead by the symbolic (a point Lacan will call a little further by *aphanisis*). (2) There is the transgression of this status of the headed subject that aims at surpassing the alienation to the Other and the subsequent effacement of the subject by the symbolic. This second movement proceeds by the negation of the Other together with their alienated subject, and an extraction of the Other's jouissance experienced as a pain inflicted by the Other. (3) This second movement implicates the third status of the headless subject that is to be located at the level of the sign rather than that of the signifier, and cannot be caught by signification, it is a symbolic death of the subject. And a death by which the Other loses the jouissance that was inscribed in them, the lost symbolic subject being the object of their demand. Furthermore, what is properly performed by this return of the drive, as opposed to the trajectory followed by the split subject's desire, and which Lacan shows us by the disquisition on Sartrean gaze, is a fabrication or a crafting of the object *a*.

Lacan next proposes in the seminar the final formalization of the two movements of the drive in a duality that goes as far as mimicking the Hegelian duality of estrangement and deestrangement (Hegel 2018, 99). Where he showed to us the montage of the drive, he tells us there is "alienation" (Lacan 1981, 212). This alienation, as in Hegel's master-slave dialectics, he tells us, is inherent to the choice of life: "your freedom or your life!" as posed before the slave in their battle to death with the master (Lacan 1981, 212). If the slave chooses freedom, they lose both life and freedom, and if they choose life they lose freedom and thereby become alienated to the master. In other words, if the subject choose satisfaction—that is their freedom—they lose life insofar as they would be choosing their death for the biological function of reproduction. And if they choose life, they would have adhered to the montage whereby their alienation to the Other is realized. What occurs in this alienation, Lacan tells us, is a submission to the law of the signifier by which the subject gets represented but also effaced by the signifier. This effacement of the subject by their representation in the Other is what Lacan calls aphanisis, a term he borrows from Ernest Jones to apply on the effect of the signifier. In short, if aphanisis for Jones is the vanishing of sexual desire, for Lacan it is the vanishing of the point of enunciation (of the subject of enunciation) by its mutation by enunciation into a subject of the enounced—that is henceforth in the Other, in effect of the Other, and thereby alienated to the Other (Lacan 1981, 210).

To direct us onto the second movement that counters this aphanisis in alienation, Lacan reminds us that the slave's initial condition—your freedom or your life!—is in fact "freedom or death" (Lacan 1981, 213). And this is a condition in which "the only proof of freedom that you can have [he tells us] is precisely to choose death, for there, you show that you have freedom of choice" (Lacan 1981, 213). We must underline here the *showing* that is involved—"you show that you have freedom of choice." In other words, this second choice of death to show freedom is a refusal of both choices if not of the dialectic altogether. And from this opening, Lacan introduces to us the second operation of the drive—as the second choice, or the nonchoice—as an antidote to alienation and an objection to aphanisis, an operation he calls separation (Lacan 1981, 214). In separation, Lacan tells us, the subject intends to engender themself, to deestrange themself from the Other their choice of life alienates them to. Now, this separation takes place, Lacan explains, in the lack of the Other—that is, the lack between signifiers—the function by which the discourse of the Other is subsumed or attributed to a desire of the Other, the lack by which the Other is rendered a desiring Other and thereby a subjectivized Other (Lacan 1981, 214–18). And it is from this desire, from the Other as desire whose object is the subject themself, that the subject may now separate by betting on their own symbolic death as a condition of their freedom of choice: if the Other desires me, if I am the object they lack, then my death equates my freedom (Lacan 1981, 214). Lacan writes: "The subject [...] comes back, then, to the initial point, which is that of his lack as such, of the lack of his aphanisis" (Lacan 1981, 219). It is in those terms that Lacan formalizes for us the two stages of the dialectic of the drive and the Other: it sets out from the lack as such—that is the lack of the subject in their function of reproduction—to bring about an alienation whereby the subject enters representation and aphanisis by the same token, then operates a separation by which the subject returns to their *lack as such* yet symbolically, for their death for the Other is a symbolic death that comes to counter their death by the symbolic. Therefore, separation doesn't lead back to the point the dialectic of subjectivation departs from, but to a renewal of the entry into alienation, and thereby to the cyclical functioning of the drive.

The dialectic of the drive and the Other can neither get back to an original presubjective point that precedes it, nor can it reach a final point of an accomplished subjectivity that is fully separate from the Other. It is a dialectic that can neither reach beginning nor end. It is a suspension of the subject in the condition whereby being, on one side of the equation, and nonbeing, on the other side, are always present in correlation. Where there is satisfaction, there is death in the biological function of reproduction; where there is symbolic subject, there is aphanisis; and where there is a headless subject, there is symbolic death. And this is pretty much the condition there is in the proposition "your freedom or your life!"—not lacking *being* somewhere in the equation is not a choice.

Yet, although Lacan considers that this is already beyond Hegel insofar as it surpasses the function of recognition in the master-slave dialectic, where his argument leads us, in fact, is to the heart of Hegelian grounds, to the very condition that Hegel formalizes as a dialectic, and which has no without. Ray Brassier concentrates this exclusivity of the dialectic—as universe—in a single-cutting argument he delivers toward the end of his article "Strange Sameness": "Externalization [of estrangement] is deestrangement as estrangement. The prospect of deestrangement emerges only by retrospecting an enabling estrangement. Objectification and subjection are facets of a single indivisible movement. This is why there can be no narrative about overcoming the need to overcome; no history in which the compulsion to repeat would be undone by the rememoration of compulsion. There is no self-relation uncontaminated by estrangement" (Brassier 2019, 104).

Brassier's conclusion on the dialectic of estrangement doesn't only summarize the endpoint of Lacan's formalization of the drive but also the kernel of Freud's revision of the duality of the drive by Empedocles's theory in his response to Ferenczi: "there can be no narrative about overcoming the need to overcome," there is neither initial nor final state where overcoming can become unnecessary or accomplished.

To return to "Analysis Terminable and Interminable," Freud starts by explaining that Empedocles had posited that the universe was organized according to two governing forces—love and strife—that are very similar to Eros and Thanatos (Freud 1964, 246). And the central opposition that love and strife sustain is not simply being and nonbeing, or life and death, but combination and dissolution. In other words, Freud tells us that there isn't in psychic life such a thing as a fully consumed death, or a stable ontological life, as the misreading of his dualistic theory of drives has drawn. All there is, is the in between—of life and death—which requires, then, combination and separation to sustain: "The one strives to agglomerate the primal particles of the four elements into a single unity, while the other, on the contrary, seeks to undo all those fusions and to separate the primal particles of the elements from one another" (Freud 1964, 246).

Those two phenomena, Freud continues, occur—according to Empedocles—in a cyclical manner: "A continuous, never-ceasing alternation of periods, in which the one or the other of the two fundamental forces gain the upper hand, so that at one time love and at another strife puts its purpose completely into effect and dominates the universe, after which the other, vanquished, side asserts itself and, in its turn, defeats its partner" (Freud 1964, 246).

We may consider, retroactively from Lacan's course on the drive, that Freud's reference to Empedocles—that shifts the operation of the drive from cycles of life-death to cycles of combination-dissolution or estrangement-deestrangement—is a fundamental course correction, and one step further indeed: for in combination, what the drive operates, we may call now alienation; and in dissolution what it operates is separation. In this sense, Empedocles's love and strife are the departure and the return of the drive in its cyclical dialectic with the Other.

Now, to put his argument back in the context of his debate with Ferenczi, Freud's very long response leads us to the idea that if truth (as Ferenczi calls it)—the essence of the subject—is in natural satisfaction, as Ferenczi posits, there would not be a subject to proclaim it as truth, it wouldn't be subjectivized. This truth is only reachable by the negation of alienation, and it is bound to lead back to alienation. What Freud puts in the mouth of Empedocles is that the essence of the subject can neither be an original nor a final state for analysis to reach, a state that is ulterior or posterior to the dialectic of the symbolic and the real. If there is such a thing as an essence, Freud tells us, it can only be conceived as the suspended horizon of negation—a first negation by alienation (love), then a second negation by separation (strife), which in turn can only lead back to the renewal of first negation. In this respect, what Freud tells us is: because the essence of the subject that Ferenczi defends is only conceivable as a part of the dialectic of self-estrangement, there can be no end to repetition—specifically, the repetition of the Other's failure insofar as it returns on the subject with their own jouissance. It is there that Freud's introduction of the drive through the question of masochism—as part of normality—takes full effect. The Other must fail again for subjectivity to persist.

Furthermore, the whole procedure by which Freud devotedly revises and defends this position suggests that truth for him, after all, is the dialectic itself. And this is, perhaps, what he considers to be the nature of the result of analysis: not something of the kind of a subjective anchoring in an original lost essence or freedom, which we have seen him meticulously reinscribe within the dialectic of alienation, but rather something at the

satisfaction. What the analysand is convinced of is that analysis "doesn't bring him anything in reality," this emphasis on the real should indicate for us that Ferenczi speaks of a sort of traversal of desire's function—that is not to reach satisfaction—whereby the analysand becomes rather tolerant to satisfaction. In that, for what concerns transference, what Ferenczi proposes to us is a modification of the analysand's enjoyment whereby the analytic situation, as modality of enjoyment, is exhausted: "the analysis must so to say die out of exhaustion"—an exhaustion that, following Ferenczi's reasoning, we should be able to call with more precision the exhaustion of fantasy and desire (Ferenczi 1982, 51).

Once there, however, Ferenczi introduces a phrase that provides context retroactively to the whole reasoning he proposed earlier: "The whole of the neurotic period of his life appears then, truly, as a pathological mourning that the patient wanted also to displace on the situation of transference, but whose veritable nature is unmasked, which puts then an end to the tendency of repetition in the future. The analytic renunciation corresponds therefore to the actual resolution of situations of infantile frustrations which were the origin of the symptomatic formations" (Ferenczi 1982, 52).

Ferenczi's foundational idea is in the master signifier "mourning"—a term that has become widespread in analytical theories since the days of this debate, if not before, and which one may clearly identify as the concept that the works of Melanie Klein had inherited. This is a term that also took center stage in the works of some Lacanian analysts, such as Daniel Lagache, and which Lacan has done enough to repudiate by the distinction between the partial object and the primordial object introduced in the concept of the object *a*. We shall see a little further how Freud's response prepares a "mourning" of the theory of mourning that Lacan will formalize later on; for now, let us try to grasp what Ferenczi advances here.

Originally, he tells us, there are "infantile frustrations" and their antidote (result)—"symptomatic formations." In other words, the symptom's business is to prevent the accomplishment of a loss to keep frustration at a bearable level. This symptom is that which he previously unfolded in the demand of the object of need, the demand of love, and the desire of the phallic object that the analysand must come to recognize. Those are the main constituents, for Ferenczi, of the "pathological mourning"—that is to say the mourning that doesn't reach "renunciation"—by which the subject counters infantile frustrations.

This means that renunciation, for Ferenczi, together with castration, means separation; and that "the tendency of repetition"—in line with symptomatic formations—is the tendency of repetition of demand, inasmuch as (for him as well) demand sustains alienation (which this logic of object-relation reduces to attachment). And it is only on those bases—that repetition is the sustainment of attachment to counter loss—that Ferenczi can posit that transference is repetition, and that, therefore, mourning and renunciation can resolve transference, repetition, and infantile frustrations by the same token.

One must point out here though that this placement of repetition on the side of alienation provides the exact opposite definition of that which Freud advances; for Freud, repetition is Empedocles's strife—it is the Other's failure—that is separation, and that is at a clear distance from transference. This is the—long-inherited—misunderstanding in response to which Lacan announces his formalization of repetition (in Seminar XI), as a fundamental concept that is distinct from transference, by the clear statement: "the concept of repetition has nothing to do with the concept of transference" (Lacan 1981, 33). It is here that we may say with assurance that the clinic of mourning is not Freudian, insofar as it stems from a notion of transference that is explained by a notion of repetition, and which are both distinct from the concepts of repetition and transference that Freud proposed.

Now, aside from those conceptual problems in Ferenczi's use of transference as repetition, and of repetition as sustainment of attachment, which remain effects of a more fundamental misunderstanding, let us turn to the master signifier (mourning) that is at the origin of all that before moving to Freud's response on this very signifier: What is it in the order of things that one can mourn? What is it, other than that whose presence precedes his absence? If there is any reason for us to believe in the necessity of such a mourning, it stems from our belief that the object is originally a positive object, and consequently that the only entry point to this business of its negativization is privation. In that, the whole purpose and natural end of analysis that Ferenczi unfolds for us depart from the object as defined by the evolutionary theory—that is, an object suspended between pleasure and attachment. Furthermore, to sustain the theory of mourning doesn't go without supposing that the being of the subject is ontic, that it is in itself, and that it may, if one mourns the thing till the end, be sustained by something else than a lack. In other words, for one to practice analysis as a clinic of mourning, one needs to be a firm believer in a sort of self-sufficiency of the subject.

Freud's response to this starts by underlining the existentialist-like optimism that imagines there is such a thing as a fully accomplished and consumed loss, as expressed in the acceptance of castration and explained in the metaphor of mourning. "In the paper read by [Ferenczi] in 1927 he made it a requirement that in every successful analysis those two complexes must have been mastered. I should like to add that, speaking from my own experience, I think that in this Ferenczi was asking a very great deal" (Freud 1964, 252).

Thus, Freud indicates that something in demand and desire doesn't work so much as Ferenczi wants them to for castration to become such a consumable fact. After leading us (through his revision of the drive) to the idea that the drive's business is to negate—rather than to reach pleasure—he argues against Ferenczi's claim that demand is a demand of love: the analysand "refuses to subject him-self to a father-substitute, or to feel indebted to him or anything" (Freud 1964, 252). Freud writes that if the demand addressed to the Other was a demand of a positive object, or a demand of the Other (as object), what would that refusal be? In other words, Freud argues that Ferenczi had classified under negative transference something that, at the end of the day, might not be so in line with a demand of the Other; that Ferenczi had neutralized, in his defense of the negative transference, a demand that longs for the exact reverse of the Other—that is to say a demand that negates the Other. After all, what is a demand of love other than a demand of the Other's lack? Freud writes: "At no other point in one's analytic work does one suffer more from an oppressive feeling that all one's repeated efforts have been in vain, and from a suspicion that one has been 'preaching to the winds,' than when one is trying to persuade a woman to abandon her wish for a penis on the ground of its being unrealizable or when one is seeking to convince a man that a passive attitude to men does not always signify castration and that it is indispensable in many relationships in life" (Freud 1964, 252).

Although what is spelled out in those lines articulates what Freud suspects to be the binding rapport there is between desire and castration, the level at which he addresses this rapport is the level of demand, and a demand to which one cannot but fail in responding. In other words, this relation of desire to castration is subsumed in an impossible demand addressed to the analyst, a demand in consequence of which the Other is bound to fail. What is demanded is the Other's failure, the Other's castration. Freud's statement exceeds by far a theoretical claim that castration anxiety is unsurpassable, it is a statement of suffering, a last plea of a condemned, whose function is to preserve a last trace to a secret. Freud tells us: at no other point in one's analytic work had I suffered as much from being—in position of the Other—negated with such persistence; at no other point had I realized that what the analysand truly demands is a nonrecovery, a nonobject, and a non-Other. And that, inasmuch as their recovery—the acceptance of castration—would be surrendering their jouissance to the Other: "he refuses to accept his recovery from the doctor" (Freud 1964, 252).

On this point, I must disagree with Chawki Azouri, according to whom Freud's words constitute a defense of the paternal function, whereby he restricts psychoanalysis in his order of inheritance from surpassing the father (Azouri 2015, 204). The resonance of Freud's words—"he refuses to subject him-self to a father-substitute, or to feel indebted to him or anything"—poses the exact opposite question: Has there ever been a paternal function involved, as a law, in castration? Or has castration been only accepted insofar as it sustained a father, and the desire of the father in position of the law, producing thereby repression and identification? There are, indeed, theorists of the dictate of the identification to the analyst (Balint for instance, one of Ferenczi's successors), but Freud is not one of them, even less when he shows us that the clinic of mourning is an ideologization of the Oedipus complex, by telling us that castration cannot be accepted. Is there anything better than mourning, after all, to sustain the father's desire in position of the law—which interdicts what is already impossible? For mourning bets on nothing else than the symbol, it is a rendering symbolic of what is missed; mourning, therefore, operates by and under the Name-of-the-Father, mourning sustains the Name-of-the-Father. Furthermore, mourning supposes that, in its completion, lack may be fully consummated and that the subject can exist by something else than a lack; which implies, then, the self-sufficiency of the symbolic subject, and thereby an existentialist deadlock. Freud doesn't address identification but the refusal of identification: he claims that castration doesn't function in accordance with the Oedipus complex, after all. In other words, the Oedipus complex whose endpoint is identification turns out to be a neurotic fallacy, the Oedipus complex turns out to be a symptom that the analysand drops at a certain point and "refuses to subject him-self to a father-substitute."

To return to this refusal that Freud underlines for us, Miller explains it departing from *Encore* in opposition to the pervert's position: "Lacan can be translated [in *Encore*] as saying—'the neurotic imagine that the Other demands their castration.' Where the acknowledged pervert admits the jouissance of the Other, the neurotic is […] perceptively directed before everything by what would be, on the part of the Other, the demand for his castration, that reduces the law of desire to a demand for castration" (Miller 1997, 29).

In effect, where the pervert may still exist in the acceptance of castration as "instrument of jouissance of the Other," the neurotic is effaced, and this is sufficient reason for this running aground on anxiety. As Freud shows, the neurotic refuses to surrender their jouissance to the Other by accepting castration.[9]

Miller continues:

> This is why Lacan can develop what plays out at the end of the analysis as the refusal, by the neurotic subject, to sacrifice his castration to the jouissance of the Other. It is even what explains in the paradoxical formula, by saying, "The Other does not exist for him." One can't understand more. This means—the Other does not exist for him, in the sense where only phallic jouissance matters fully. At this moment there, he refuses the sacrifice that is necessary for the Other to exist. As Lacan says, "If he existed, he would be pleasured by my castration." (Miller 1997, 29)

In this sense, one may ask if this sacrifice of knowledge is an unbeing of the supposed subject of knowledge, and in reversed reasoning, if the unbeing of this supposition is protective of jouissance. Is the unbeing of the subject of knowledge a beyond of castration? Or is it a holding on to castration that goes as far as negating the Other? We shall return to this question later on, for Lacan will tell us that castration is only the imaginary support of lack located in the third stage of the object *a*. But for now, Freud tells us that this is the final scene of an analysis, which is a scene that is phallic in appearance (a holding on to castration) but anal in kind (you won't get my jouissance). As Freud writes: "No analogous transference can arise from the female's wish for a penis, but it is the source of outbreaks of severe depression in her, owing to an internal conviction that the analysis, will be of no use and that nothing can be done to help her. And we can only agree that she is right, when we learn that her strongest motive in coming for treatment was the hope that, after all, she might still obtain a male organ, the lack of which was so painful to her" (Freud 1964, 252).

It is in those words that Freud shows us how this holding on to castration produces a disbelief in knowledge and in analysis at once, together with the realization of that desire—"her strongest motive in coming for treatment was the hope that, after all, she might still obtain a male organ"—is a lure in the sense that desire only leads back to the castration it departs from. In that, what Freud provides us is a little more detailed than Ferenczi's claim: it isn't *the crystalline structure of character* that is dissolved in that moment of analysis (for what is character?) but it is desire, for desire is castration, that is to say the Other's desire. Then it is from this point that Freud advances onto formalizing castration as a bedrock, insofar as it constitutes the last frontier of knowledge (the Other): "The decisive thing remains that the resistance prevents any change from taking place—that everything stays as it was. We often have the impression that with the wish for a penis and the masculine protest we have penetrated through all the psychological strata and have reached bedrock, and that thus our activities are at an end. This is probably true, since, for the psychical field, the biological field does in fact play the part of the underlying bedrock. The repudiation of femininity can be nothing else than a biological fact, a part of the great riddle of sex" (Freud 1964, 252).

Here, we must first question Freud's introduction of the "repudiation of femininity," which he substitutes to Alfred Adler's "masculine protest" two pages earlier (Freud 1964, 250). What difference is there between those two formulations, aside from Freud's expressed intention of accommodating *Penisneid* along with the fear of castration? If the masculine protest relates to castration from the outset of the object as positivized, if it is a reclamation of the phallus as it were prior to—or in fear of—its loss, the repudiation of femininity underlines the exact reverse, whereby the object as negativized constitutes the initial point. And if Freud precludes both, the fear of castration and *Penisneid*, in this initially negativized state of the object, then the penis is already posited to be a positivization of a lack that precedes it. In other words, what is operated by Freud's formulation and use of repudiation of femininity is not the repudiation of femininity, but the repudiation of lack, the repudiation of the negativization of the object.

Now it is this repudiation of lack that Freud tells us is a bedrock that "can be nothing else than a biological fact, a part of the great riddle of sex" (Freud 1964, 252). Why does he not stop at the biological fact in explaining this bedrock? He adds: "a part of the great riddle of sex," the riddle that constitutes enjoyment in both men and women. Freud doesn't hide his disappointment here, for what is it that one calls a riddle other than that which he hasn't found a knowledge about—in the unconscious—and which he dumps, therefore, in the "biological fact" that is unformalizable? Is that not what is meant by this bedrock? Is it not, precisely, a *bedrock* in what concerns signification? Miller interprets this disappointment of Freud in the following: "what did Freud expect of the experience if not a formula for the sexual relation? He hoped to find it inscribed in the unconscious; hence his despair at not finding it" (Miller 2009, 2). In that, one may say that Lacan's breakthrough in Seminar X, where he addresses lack as *irreducible to a signifier*, isn't so strange to this experience of disappointment Freud tells us about; it is a formalization of this dead end that Freud delivers to us in vivo.

In conclusion, I have proposed five antitheses against the theory of mourning—that is, to be more specific, a mourning of the partial object. Allow me to summarize these antitheses by briefly correlating them to the formalizations that Lacan will bring to them. (1) Freud tells us that demand is deception insofar as it aims at the Other's lack, and thereby that demand is separation, not alienation; and this is a point Lacan will formalize in Seminar X under *that which deceives*. (2) Freud shows us that the paternal function is an effect of castration, not a cause of castration (as in the Oedipus complex); which is a rupture with the Oedipus complex Lacan will conceptualize by a rerouting of castration in detumescence—the anatomical falling out of phallic representation of the male organ at the moment of reaching jouissance. (3) Freud shows us that if the analysand, after all, "refuses to subject him-self to a father-substitute," then the paternal function is in itself a positivization of the lacking object; and this is an idea Lacan will develop in the object's entry into exchange by the medium of the castration complex. (4) Freud tells us that desire leads nowhere other than castration; which Lacan will formalize in that desire can only lead back to lack, which renders the object a lack *cause of desire*, as opposed to an *object of desire*. And finally (5), Freud shows us that the repudiation of femininity—that is the repudiation of lack—is the bedrock of formalization; which Lacan will translate into the irreducible lack, the lack that is irreducible to a signifier. These are the five antitheses by which Freud counters the theory of mourning, as a guiding principle of analysis, whose endpoint is a full acceptance of castration.

These are, moreover, five of the fundamental coordinates of the object as object *a*. And one must therefore point out that although Lacan challenges Freud on the end of analysis—on so many occasions in Seminar X (1962–1963)—Lacan must have followed to the letter Freud's antitheses as theoretical indications in some cases, and as evidences in others, calling for a conceptualization such as the object *a*. It is by the object *a* and its fourth stage after all that Lacan will show us how *mourning* cannot realize more than a substitution, since what may be mourned is the object as seen (its image *i(a)*, which is already a substitute) and not the object as seeing (the gaze). So, this falling of the gaze involves a destitution that exceeds mourning, and that is to situate rather on the opposite side of mourning, in melancholia. Why would Ferenczi qualify, at the end of the day, such a thing as the dissolution of the crystalline structure of character as a mourning? The whole emphasis in this dissolution is on destitution rather than loss. Ferenczi's practice—which opposes his concept—is what's beyond mourning, as we will see in the third chapter.

A Cut, a Fall, and the Finitude of Finitude

And this leads to the final point, the cut. At no point in "Analysis Terminable and Interminable" does it seem, despite so many of Freud's theoretical reconsiderations, that Freud is losing ground on a particular certainty. There is one single thing that is out of the question from beginning to end, one certainty that he is not willing to negotiate with anyone, anywhere in the lines of this article. This point that we have seen, first introduced in the symptom not to interpret, then operationalized in the economy of the unsynthesizable, then drawn so well in the defense of the drive by Empedocles's theory, and finally substantiated in the five antitheses against the concept of mourning, we will see now this certainty is the cut.

And although Freud never quoted Hegel, or even read him as far as we know, his certainty is phenomenological insofar as what he is certain of is that the ethical can at no point become ontic, no matter how well has it been treated by negation. What Freud is certain of, to go back to Brassier's formalization, is that "there can be no narrative about overcoming the need to overcome; [thus] there is no self-relation uncontaminated by estrangement" (Brassier 2019, 104). In fact, Ferenczi provides such a narrative, but then the narrative itself is a fact of the need to overcome, of which it narrates the overcoming. In fact, Freud tells us not to bother searching there for a purpose to analysis, for what can be found in this transcendental realm—that Ferenczi's conceptualization provides—does not exceed psychotherapy. Any concept of a finality to psychoanalysis must align with this impossibility that he shows us the analysand coming to realize, at the turning point of their analysis, in what he calls an "internal conviction." According to Freud, "No analogous transference can arise from the female's wish for a penis, but it is the source of outbreaks of severe depression in her, owing to an internal conviction that the analysis, will be of no use and that nothing can be done to help her. And we can only agree that she is right, when we learn that her strongest motive in coming for treatment was the hope that, after all, she might still obtain a male organ" (Freud 1964, 252).

Does Freud go as far as claiming that transference can be liquidated? As a matter of fact, Freud only speaks of a resolution of the transference neurosis—never a liquidation—when he doesn't address what this resolution really involves; he introduces this resolution in most of his writings as a gateway to another articulation, but never addresses it as a problem itself—this also occurs in the beginning of this very essay we are reading (Freud 1964, 218). Now, the quote we have before us here is clearly distinct from this usual dismissive affirmation of the resolution of the transference neurosis. Freud doesn't venture in such a claim here, he rather approaches the question of transference comparatively—"no analogous transference can arise"—as if there is something in transference that doesn't allow such a clear distinction on the matter, as the one there is in a resolution. And although this inability to distinguish may stem from Freud's limited understanding of castration and the feminine position (which we will address in the third chapter) Freud's comparative approach also poses the question of whether transference is limited to, or produced by, the analytic situation, for this analytic situation to assume such a responsibility as that of resolving it. In other words, this comparative approach—that is opposed to the idea of the resolution of transference—poses the question of whether there is a subjective rapport that, as strange from analysis as it can be, is exterior to transference. On that, Freud claims, as early as in *Five Lectures on Psycho-Analysis (1909)*, that "transference arises spontaneously in all human relationships just as it does between the patient and the physician," so the "myth" of the resolution of transference loses its conceptual ground quite early in the history of psychoanalysis (Freud 2000–2010, 2236). Now, I am certainly not claiming that what Freud advances here, which is a passage *à l'acte* as will become clear in the third chapter, is the last thing that could happen to a transference in analysis (and out of it of course); but I am pointing out that Freud is approaching transference quite correctly, he is speaking in terms of what is realizable, a "nonanalogousness" of transference—as opposed to a transcendence of transference.

There can be "no analogous transference" to that which was sustained, Freud claims, by the "wish for the partial object" along the analytic treatment, and which falls, at the end, by the medium of an "internal conviction." So what Freud tells us already is that transference doesn't end, it subsists, but not without a cut that is this "internal conviction," in effect of which transference subsists nonanalogously. This is far more delicate and nuanced than what Ferenczi proposes by telling us about the "feeling of equality in relation to the physician," and the "far clearer separation of fantasy from reality, obtained by analysis" (Ferenczi 1982, 47–51). And here I should like to point out the nuance again, that although Ferenczi has led analysis beyond Freud, Freud's conceptual delicacy maintains a greater sobriety, or immunity, against the ideological and transcendental outcome of analysis that was derived from Ferenczi's claims—especially regarding transference. For if one thinks transference at the end of analysis through this "equality in relation to the physician," or the "clearer separation of fantasy from reality," or, even better, the "internal freedom that is quasi unlimited," one cannot but end up in the idea of the resolution of transference—which stems from the very misunderstanding of transference (Ferenczi 1982, 47).

Now let us approach this "internal conviction," the central element of the proposition, Freud tells us he "can only agree she is right" in. What internal conviction does Freud agree the analysand is right in? Is it that she will not obtain a male organ after all? Or that her analysis had been motivated by this desire all along? Or that, after this conviction, analysis has become useless? Isn't "conviction" a rather strange word to be used in such a domain? Have we ever seen this word written in a psychoanalytic text—other than Freud's and Ferenczi's texts on the end of analysis? Doesn't Freud tell us, by naming this an "internal conviction," that something has gotten out of hand? Does he not tell us that this analysand is all alone in her conviction? That he does not share with her this same conviction, but that in a certain way—the way of the evident perhaps—he gets forced to agree? Does he not tell us that by this conviction the internal has gotten concealed again for him, in the sense that conviction doesn't demand recognition? It is so strange that he who has led analysis as far as destitution—Ferenczi—hasn't given us a single word on the unbeing of the supposed subject of knowledge, for he dumps it all in negative transference, while what Freud tells us in all the fury of this passage *à l'acte* is that it was all about his destitution as subject of knowledge.

To be convinced, after all, is neither being certain nor needing to know; and Descartes is accountable enough by his creation of the nondeceiving God out of his first certainty for how demanding certainty is in its relation to knowledge, inasmuch as it aims at truth (Lacan 1981, 36). The conviction that Freud tells us about, and that he qualifies as internal, is something else, it is of a different category than that by which Descartes had to get rid of God (if I reached the certainty that "I am" by pure reason, then God wants me to) and which since Lacan has been called a sleight of hand. The analysand's conviction Freud tells us about at that point did not assume that the Other agrees, but it forced him to, it gave him no other choice: he "can only agree that she is right," that the right is in her. Doesn't that involve the Other's becoming a lack? For what else does this conviction lead Freud to than lacking conviction? Doesn't this conviction preclude a stumbling of the Other, a fall, up to a certain extent? The very last lines of Freud's article are astonishingly precise on this matter. He doesn't only tell us that the Other falls with his knowledge or "mastery" (as he calls it using Ferenczi's words, "the mastery of the castration complex"), which requires then that he "consoles" himself with something, but also that what he falls into, or back to, is "certainty"—that is, his position of divided subject: "It would be hard to say whether and when we have succeeded in mastering this factor [the repudiation of femininity] in analytical treatment. We can only console ourselves with the certainty that we have given the person analyzed every possible encouragement to examine and alter her attitude to it" (Freud 1964, 252).

What Freud tells us, now that all is said and done, is that he doesn't know, but he is certain. And what does his certainty account for, what is he certain of other than the will he places against his doubt? In other words, he is back on the couch, divided. To return to the conviction, that is the suspended evidence inseparable from experience and irreducible to knowledge, one can see it laid out in the same lines Mladen Dolar writes to explain Hegel's absolute knowledge:

> One could say that the absolute knowledge is a crossroad, a partition. There are two ways that follow from it: having reached this point, having climbed to the top of this ladder, one can only revert to the experience, which was there all along—the way to truth is truth itself, the absolute knowledge is nothing but the realization that the truth was produced on the way, unwittingly, and that there is nothing more to learn there, no wisdom to possess

(this is, by the way, why Kojève's talk about "the Hegelian sage" is nonsense), except for what has been learned on the way. (Dolar 2017, 88)

Isn't this absolute knowledge the internal conviction—in its three propositions combined—that Freud told us to be "the source of outbreaks of severe depression in her"? (1) That there is nowhere else to go from there, other than to the beginning; (2) that truth, after all, is what she already experienced; and (3) that there was nothing else left for her to learn? Is there not in this absolute knowledge the very failure of knowledge as supposed, the failure of the "male organ" (to stick to Freud's words) whose absence is projected on infinity? Dolar's further explanation of the function of the cut produced by absolute knowledge—that he already compares to the end of analysis—interprets with great precision the nuance that Freud introduced in the axiom "internal conviction, ergo non-analogousness of transference": "The absolute knowledge thus rejoins the sense certainty, the most naïve beginning of the *Phenomenology*, experience is caught in a circle, one is thrown back on one's own experience, on its beginning—yet with a cut, after the break produced by the absolute knowledge. Is there life after the absolute knowledge? The parallel has been already suggested a number of times: it is like continuing to live one's life after analysis, after the break produced by analysis, and the absolute knowledge is in structural analogy with the end of analysis" (Dolar 2017, 88).

Although supporting absolute knowledge by the end of analysis might not surpass elucidation—for if anyone could testify and give evidence on the end of analysis, that doesn't make it more graspable than absolute knowledge—Dolar's comparison permits the reverse. Can absolute knowledge support the end of analysis in its conceptualization? What Dolar tells us is that absolute knowledge is, on the one hand, the cut in knowledge by which experience gets disentangled from it and starts leading back to itself ("the sense certainty, the most naïve beginning of the *Phenomenology*"), and on the other hand, the cut in experience to which experience is led back to, in itself—that is an opening in experience that leads "from consciousness to subject," out of itself, and thereby to logic (Dolar 2017, 88). So, this cut is, in fact, a departure from knowledge as supposed (in consciousness), that is, at the same time, an entry into knowledge as produced (in subject), but all that, in a closure of experience on itself in infinite cycles.

The critical fact that Dolar questions, at this point of his article, is how experience becomes *estranged* from itself while realizing its fall into repetition and similarity to itself; how it becomes "nonanalogous transference," to use Freud's words, while continuing to function as transference. Dolar explains this nonanalogousness of experience after absolute knowledge by two factors: absolute knowledge leads to a recognition (1) that experience repeats experience in cycles, that experience is but a loop there is no way out of, and (2) that experience is "subtended" by a cut in experience, whose opening submits it to a logic out of itself (Dolar 2017, 88). These are, indeed, Hegel's two scars on experience by absolute knowledge—that are not so distinct from Freud's—in sequence with which Dolar asks: "Is there life after the absolute knowledge?" Hegel tells us there is *the pure decision to think*, which Dolar translates into there is "the life of the concept" (Dolar 2017, 89).

Should we ask the same question about the end of analysis? Is there life after the end of analysis? This is a far more complex question than the first, for Freud doesn't tell us "there is the life of the concept," he tells us "there is and there isn't" life after analysis—he tells us there is "Analysis Terminable and Interminable." At one pole of the article, he writes, "no analogous transference can arise from the female's wish for a penis," and at the other he writes, "what analysis achieves for neurotics is nothing other than what normal people [who are not excluded from this wish for a penis] bring about for themselves"—which is then a temporary solution to a temporary strength of the drive (Freud 1964, 225–52). Freud's constant perplexity when approaching this question of the end of analysis—for any answer to the question must consider the duality of "Analysis [is] Terminable and [is] Interminable"—shows us that the true question he was burdened by is not, "does analysis have an end?" but, "what is the termination of analysis an end of?" What is it in the order of ends that analysis terminable must realize, and thereby become, without resentment, interminable? What Freud was asking, with all the sharpness of the experimental neurology he departed from, is, "What is it an end of, that reduces the terminality of analysis to a negligible factor, in approaching the question of the end of analysis?" This is the question that Freud has finally opened for us, by the internal conviction that equates absolute knowledge.

"The end" is a term that is not without a long philosophical history, which I certainly cannot sufficiently address in this chapter. I shall only approach it very briefly in Hegel's phenomenology with the aim of deducing Freud's answer to the question, whose final formulation in "Analysis Terminable and Interminable" I have just uncovered. This spine for "the end," which Rebecca Comay and Frank Ruda extracted in (and from) *The Dash*, is in the question of whether there is such a thing as an ended end, whether there is a final and fully consumed end, or if the end—as Hegel shows us—is an un-end "forcing us not only to begin anew but to think of beginning in a new way" (Comay and Ruda 2018, 109). And this is what Freud had been telling us with his long section on the drive, and more specifically by Empedocles's theory, that there is no separation that one can conceive of as final, there is no final end, there are only different entries to repetition. This leads to the second point, which Alenka Zupančič explains with the idea that the end and repetition (just like desire and castration) are one and the same thing in the sense that repetition is driven by the end (repetition seeks the end) and therefore the end is cause of repetition (Zupančič 2016, 1). The third point that Zupančič offers before concluding her article is crucial for understanding Freud's answer to the question:

> The fact that there are real causes of concern here [in Zeno's obsession with health] (if concern it is) in no way contradicts the fantasmatic character of many of these representations of the end. What I mean by this is that the idea of even the most radical, definitive, irreversible End serves as a framework through which we contemplate (and interpret) our present reality; and it often serves as means of its ideological consolidation. It serves, first, to give us an idea of just how much is needed to change our present reality, that is, it provides a spectacular answer to the question: what has to end in order for our present troubles to end? (Zupančič 2016, 8)

Zupančič's formulation of "the end" as framework, perhaps of fantasy as such, insofar as fantasy is the kernel of desire's positivization of lack, allows us to posit now that what Freud describes as radically lost in the analysand's "internal conviction"—the cut of absolute knowledge—is nothing other than this framework, this idea of the final end. Let us read Freud's thesis one more time: "No analogous transference can arise from the female's wish for a penis, but it is the source of outbreaks of severe depression in her, owing to an internal conviction that the analysis, will be of no use and that nothing can be done to help her" (Freud 1964, 252).

It is the internal conviction that there isn't a final end that analysis can reach—"analysis will be of no use and that nothing can be done to help her"—whereby this suffering of hers can be done with once and for all. So what is it an end of that reduces the terminality of analysis to a negligible factor in approaching the question of the end of analysis? Is it not the end of the one and final end? The only possible end to analysis, Freud tells us, inasmuch as end is repetition, is the end of the one and final end; in which case the cut of absolute knowledge would have elucidated that the end has already taken place, and that it will continue to do so indefinitely. This is the only logic—which is Hegel's logic—able to give sense to "Analysis Terminable and Interminable," analysis may be considered as terminated when it has become interminable, when it has ended the idea of its final end.

Notes

1. Freud uses the concept of ego instead of character, all along his paper, to counter the thesis proposed by Ferenczi on the reconstitution of character.
2. *Trieb* is mistranslated in the text as *instinct* instead of *drive.*
3. I refer to the concept of the drive here, departing from Freud's dualistic theory of drives in "Beyond the Pleasure Principle," where he takes the compulsion to repeat as evidence in order to posit pleasure as being the obstacle for the drives rather than their object. My use of this concept of drives equally refers to Lacan's formalization of Freud's duality of drives (in Seminar X and Seminar XI) in a single drive whose duality is brought down to the stages of its functioning: alienation and separation. In the section "The Drive as Negation" of Chap. 2, I bring together those two concepts of the drive through close reading Freud's use of Empedocles' theory of love and strife in "Analysis Terminable and Interminable."

4. Although surplus jouissance is a concept Lacan derives from Marx's concept of surplus value to define the aim of the drive beyond pleasure, I intend to show here how Freud's reasoning on the economy of the drive (given the impossibility of synthesis he advances as evidence) hinted already to the economic deadlock that requires this formalization, in continuity to his conceptualization of the drive as a death drive in "Beyond the Pleasure Principle." An exhaustive explanation of the concept of surplus jouissance is provided in the section "The Drive as Negation" of Chap. 2.
5. Lacan's differentiation of ego and subject within Freud's use of the notion of ego refers to his distinction between Freud's subject of primary narcissism (that Lacan complements by his early works on the mirror stage) and the subject of desire (which Lacan substantiates as a "lack of being"). This distinction will be addressed abundantly in Chap. 4, "Impossible Transference and the Cartesian Prospect," from Lacan's reference to Descartes on the subject of enunciation and the subject of the enounced to his final contribution on the matter in *La Logique du Fantasme*.
6. My use of the term "imaginary" refers to Lacan's early works on the mirror stage and his formalization of imaginary recognition as a misrecognition, provided it is subtended by an identification to the ideal-ego (the image of completeness, the gestalt whereby the subject defend themself against their division). The "imaginary other" is used here as a synonym to "ideal-ego" which the subject can only relate to as oppression, as opposed to the alienation that is the proper of the "symbolic Other" (ego-ideal, or big Other) as locus of truth that sustains the subject rather as a subject than as an ego. The intertwining of imaginary and symbolic will be thoroughly investigated in the section "Impossible Transference and the Cartesian Prospect" of Chap. 4.
7. Lacan calls this an "obsessive inversion."
8. Although the debate on the practical termination of treatment takes place in the shades of Ferenczi's unfinished analysis with Freud, that is a dimension I will not address for the moment. However, we must underline that Ferenczi's argument, conceptually speaking, was a binding one: *"Analysis is not an endless process, but one which can be brought to a natural end with sufficient skill and patience on the analyst's part"* (Ferenczi 1982, 53). This means that except in the case of analysis being inhibited by the analyst's resistances, it should reach its natural end. In other words, one can either believe that analysis has a natural end, or one is in resistance to analysis. I

do not intend, here, to assert that analysis may reach its end despite the analyst's resistances, it is certain that it cannot; what I seek is to show Freud's procedure in posing the question in pure form. Freud's passage, on the resistance of the analyst, may be considered an unbinding of the two following questions: Regardless of how well the analyst has analyzed their resistances, for "not only the therapeutic analysis of patients but [the analyst's] own analysis would change from a terminable into an interminable task" (Freud 1964, 249), and regardless of how well the analyst does not-inhibit the patient's analysis, can character-analysis reach a *natural* end? And does analysis have an end at all? This is what Freud wants to ask.

Freud works on the distinction between *therapeutic-analysis* and *character-analysis*, remarking that as long as analysis is *therapeutic*, its termination remains "*a practical matter*." For, he continues, "*Every experienced analyst will be able to recall a number of cases in which he had bidden his patient a permanent farewell rebus bene gestis [things having gone well]*" (Freud 1964, 250). On the other side, "*in cases of what is known as character-analysis there is a far smaller discrepancy between theory and practice. Here it is not easy to foresee a natural end, even if one avoids any exaggerated expectations and sets the analysis no excessive tasks*" (Freud 1964, 250). It is there that Freud asks the question in pure form—*is there an end for analysis (character-analysis) at all?*—and proceeds onto demand, desire, and castration in the final part of the article.

9. Although the conventional way to proceed here would be to pose the question of what difference there is between the results of analysis in neurosis and perversion, such trajectory can only assume that the conceptual distinction can be discerned by turning to the facts of how their analyses would end. What Freud suggests in his writing is the exact reverse of this procedure, that is, departing from the facts of the end of the neurotic's analysis to distinguish it from perversion. I chose to follow this particular path that Freud offers, all the way to its formalization by Lacan, in the remaining part of Chap. 2 as in Chap. 3, "The Perversion of Perversion."

References

Avello, José Jiménez. 2000. La métapsychologie chez Ferenczi. Pulsion de mort ou passion de mort? *Le Coq-Héron, Ferenczi et la psychanalyse contemporaine* 154: 17–25.

Azouri, Chawki. 2015. *J'ai réussi là où le paranoïaque échoue*. Toulouse: Erès.
Brassier, Ray. 2019. Strange Sameness: Hegel, Marx and the Logic of Estrangement. *Angelaki* 24 (1): 98–105.
Comay, Rebecca, and Frank Ruda. 2018. *The Dash: The Other Side of Absolute Knowing*. Cambridge, MA: MIT Press.
Dolar, Mladen. 2017. Being and MacGuffin. *Crisis and Critique* 4: 1.
Ferenczi, Sándor. 1938. *Thalassa: A Theory of Genitality*, 372–374. Translated by Henry Bunker. The Psychoanalytic Quarterly.
———. 1982. Le Problème de La Fin de L'Analyse. In *Psychanalyse IV. Œuvres Complètes 1927–1933*. Payot.
———. 1985. Projection de la Psychologie des Adultes sur les Enfants. *Journal clinique, (janvier–octobre 1932)*. Payot.
Freud, Sigmund. 1964. Analysis Terminable and Interminable. In *Moses and Monotheism, An Outline of Psycho-Analysis, and Other Works*, vol. 23 of The Standard Edition of the Complete Psychological Works of Sigmund Freud. Translated by James Strachey. London: Hogarth Press.
———. 2000–2010. Five Lectures on Psycho-Analysis. (1909). In *Freud: Complete Works*, translated and edited by Ivan Smith. https://www.valas.fr/IMG/pdf/Freud_Complete_Works.pdf.
Granoff, Wladimir. 1958. Ferenczi: faux problème ou vrai malentendu. *Psychanalyse* 6: 255–282.
Gutiérrez-Peláez, Miguel. 2015. Ferenczi's Anticipation of the Traumatic Dimension of Language: A Meeting with Lacan. *Contemporary Psychoanalysis* 51 (1): 137–154.
Hegel, Georg Wilhelm Fredrich. 2018. *The Phenomenology of Spirit*. Translated by Terry Pinkard and Michael Baur. Cambridge: Cambridge University Press.
Lacan, Jacques. 1962–1963/1981. *The Four Fundamental Concepts of Psycho-analysis*. The Seminar of Jacques Lacan, vol. XI. Edited by Jacques-Alain Miller and translated by Alan Sheridan. New York: W. W. Norton.
Miller, Jacques-Alain. 1997. The Drive is Speech. *Umbr(a): On the Drive* 1: 15–33.
———. 2009. Another Lacan. *The Symptom* 10 (Spring), 1–8.
Zupančič, Alenka. 2016. The End. *Provocations* 1: 1–19.

3

The "Rescuing" of Castration

Roberto Harari explains that "Lacan [...] rescued the concept of castration" from its interpretation by Freud as castration complex and from its reduction to mourning and renunciation by Ferenczi, which influenced the Kleinian school (Harari 2001, 1529). What Harari rightfully calls a "rescuing" is Lacan's rearticulation of castration beyond the lack of the partial object as missing jouissance. In other words, castration—beyond its imaginary function—becomes the object itself, the object lack that turns jouissance as such into its possibility, that is, in turn, that of the subject.

This articulation does not occur, however, without (1) reinscribing Freud into a Hegelian lineage. The endeavor that leads Lacan to the object *a* is still a return to Freud via Kierkegaard's work on anxiety and subjectivation. This articulation also requires (2) a serious engagement with the question of the Other's ontology as offered by Durkheim and Mauss and as later on formalized—or rather dismissed—by Lévi-Strauss and structuralism. Further, (3) this articulation is central in Lacan's amendment of psychical structures which he calls forth in Seminar X, once as evidence supporting conceptual revision, and again as concepts deriving from it. So when one considers how Lacan turns the lack of the

M. Tal, *The End of Analysis*, The Palgrave Lacan Series,
https://doi.org/10.1007/978-3-031-29889-9_3

object—and the subject with it—into the object itself, one really has to revise such a number of theoretical constituents and implications that one gets the impression that it was at that point in time that analysis was truly being conceptualized.

What requires us to address this conceptualization, and advance along Lacan's procedure in all three of those trials (starting with the most evident), is the fact that Freud leaves us with the idea that by the time an analysis has ended the object and castration are understood to be one and the same thing—a point he raises in considering castration to be the bedrock of subjectivity and announcing mourning as being an interminable affair (Freud 1964, 252). Against the readings that depart from Lacan's objections to Freud's limit to analysis—that is, Freud's confusion of the complex with castration—I shall address the object *a*, not as a beyond to Freud's running aground on castration but as the concept whereby Lacan enables us to grasp this very running aground as being a subjective destitution, the destitution from which the traversal of fantasy and the "unbeing" of the supposed subject of knowledge are to result. That is, this chapter aims to demonstrate—departing from Lacan's formalization of the object as lack—how the sole success of desire is the destitution that henceforth amends it.

The Perversion of Perversion

What "Analysis Terminable and Interminable" ends on is the idea that the neurotic's castration cannot be accepted—a conclusion Freud advances by considering the "repudiation of femininity" (Freud 1964, 252) as the bedrock of subjectivity. That Freud has chosen to leave us on such a brutal encounter with ontology cannot be dismissed, for he tells us that castration and desire are one, that desire is castration, and that repudiation is what preserves it. This repudiation of castration Freud advances as a bedrock opposes, however, a widespread idea (even within Freudian orthodoxy) that the neurotic is the only subject whose structure allows an acceptance of castration. In fact, what Freud spoke about in this regard, as early as in 1914, is the neurotic's "acknowledgment" or "recognition" of castration, which he immediately assigned to repression, and opposed to the psychotic's disavowal of castration (1925) and to the pervert's splitting of the ego (1939), wherein the disavowal and the acknowledgment of castration are concomitantly present (Freud 2000–2010b, 3589; 1925, 4151, 1940, 5008). So Freud's standpoint is not the relation of structure to castration but castration's relation to structure; the neurotic's acknowledgment of castration is a repudiation, and he doesn't get to accept castration more than that—this is Freud's very definition of neurosis.

And against the broadly dismissive attitude to this Freudian standing point—as held in many schools—one must stress that this is a proposition that is to be approached very carefully. "Neurosis is repudiation, as acknowledging relation to castration" does not mean "the neurotic cannot accept to lack the phallus," but that "there is not a without to desire—inasmuch as desire and castration are one—other than anxiety." This is the deadlock Freud stumbled upon, calling forth into the psychoanalytic literature such a strange term as "bedrock."

Let us turn our attention now to another critical fact. The axiom I deduced from "Analysis Terminable and Interminable" in the second chapter—mourning (as acceptance of castration) is only good for the pervert—doesn't perform well only for us, but also for Freud himself. A year after the publication of "Analysis Terminable and Interminable," Freud wrote "Splitting of the Ego in the Process of Defense," where he risks grounding his entire argument on a single case of perversion (Freud 2000–2010f, 5062). Why does Freud take such a risk? This is the logical consequence of his findings in "Analysis Terminable and Interminable." If mourning is only good for the pervert, then something in neurosis requires an understanding of perversion; something in neurosis must be rescued from perversion, and this is what he tries to achieve. It can be argued that "Analysis Terminable and Interminable" is nothing else than an attempt to rescue the neurotic's castration from the pervert's successful mourning.

Moreover, when did Freud ever endow castration with acceptance? When did he ever correlate those two words? The only place, in all of his Complete Works, where Freud speaks deliberately of such an acceptance of castration is where he speaks about perversion. Even there, however, he speaks about it in terms of "masochistic phantasies which were wholly derived from a wish to accept castration" (Freud 2000–2010c, 4016).

Even there, he speaks about it as a "wish," a fantasy, and one that is vital for the pervert indeed. For, as we've seen earlier, Lacan points out that the only subject who accepts castration, insomuch as castration turns their jouissance into the Other's, is the pervert—and that, insofar as the Other's jouissance is theirs. That is why the pervert never bluff when they speak as law, for it is as Other that they enjoy.

Where the pervert cannot be mistaken, in fact, is in their tyranny against perversion, the perversion they generate all around them, the one they make us believe to be a perversion. The pervert is not they who dwell in sin (this is the neurotic) but they who legislate its punishment. And the pervert does so on the prerequisite of fixing the inherent malfunctioning of jouissance by accepting castration to enjoy as Other. Lacan explains this fundamental characteristic of the perverse position in the following terms:

> If we know something now about the pervert, it is that what appears from the outside to be an unbounded satisfaction is actually a defense and an implementation of a law inasmuch as it curbs, suspends, and halts the subject on the path to jouissance. For the perverts, the will to jouissance is, as for anyone else, a will that fails, that encounters its own limit, its own reining-in, in the very exercise of desire. [...] The pervert doesn't know what jouissance he is serving in exercising his activity. It is not, in any case, in the service of his own jouissance. (Lacan 2014, 150)

This is a concept of perversion that precedes Freud by more than a century, Freud only stumbles on it by the end of his life, and Lacan formulates it for us here, but Hegel had already advanced a substantial treatment of perversion in the evil consciousness (Hegel 2018, 385).

All that certainly poses the question of whether the pervert's acceptance is, in fact, not the most inaccessible disavowal of castration there could be. It poses the question of whether it really is *castration* that the pervert accepts or rather the castration complex—for the pervert's Other is pure enjoyment.

The pervert, to give them back what is theirs, "wishes to ignore [the symbolic father] because it requires him to acknowledge the lack in the Other," as Joël Dor explains. Dor considers therefore that "the lacking mother desires the father only because he is not without the phallus," as opposed to her desiring sexual difference—and thereby lack as such (Dor 2001, 104). We must be very attentive here to Dor's words. Dor—who is a Lacanian—speaks about the pervert with the very same Oedipal terminology that Freud used to speak about the neurotic. She tells us that the pervert thinks that what is both lacked and desired is well and truly a phallus—a positive object—which makes castration a horror for him, a bloody imaginary castration whose business is the bypassing of lack as such (Dor 2001, 104). For as soon as lack is encountered by him, it is positivized as phallus in the Other, the Other which the pervert posits has taken it. In other words, insofar as castration for the pervert is strictly a bloody exchange of the phallus, which plays as a modality of its preservation, castration for the pervert is fantasy, and a very well-known one, of course—the Oedipal castration complex itself. So the main point, here is that Freud approached neurosis using a theory about perversion (and I showed how Freud realized it doesn't work) according to which the neurotic is in fact distinct from the pervert and according to which the Oedipal complex serves a perverse fantasy. And this ended up in the fact that mourning was a not less fantastic fact than the complex it stems from. Following from that, one may refer to Lacan's incisive statement, in Seminar X that "the castration of the complex is not a castration" but the object's entry into exchange (Lacan 2014, 89–90).

So let us give back to the pervert what belongs to the pervert and consider him as a first criterion of subjectivation out of which Lacan will rescue the second criterion—that is, the neurotic's *Heim*. The Oedipus complex—whose starting point is in the threat of a bloody castration and endpoint is in the Other's jouissance (identification)—is the pervert's fantasy, which they are in fact the only to implement fully. The Oedipus complex is by no means a neurotic foundation; it is a perverse fantasy that is only used by the neurotic and in a very limited manner. Let us also add to that, in response to a very widespread belief that is rooted in the Oedipal complex, and that posits that perversion is a sort of nonaccess to identification (as an "exit" from, or "resolution" of the complex), that identification is perversion at its purest—for its sole gratification is the Other's enjoyment. Only the pervert enjoys as Other. So, to straighten things out, we must see that a successful resolution of the Oedipal complex—as long as resolution means identification[1]—is nothing but the establishment of perversion. Therefore, mourning is only good for the pervert, as I said, and with it identification.

To take one last but fundamental axiom from Dor's treatment of perversion before picking up Lacan's extraction of *Heim*, "this fantasy [that is the castration complex] makes him [the pervert] renounce the assumption of his own desire, beyond castration" for "only the renunciation of the primal object of desire safeguards the possibility of desire itself" (Dor 2001, 104–5). This is the cutting rift there is between the neurotic and the pervert. The pervert has an object of desire (a positive primal object) and thus does not have a desire, while the neurotic has an object cause of desire (i.e., a negative object, a lack in the Other) that is an object where they stand in a position of cause to their desire.

This is the structural rift, in fact, where Lacan lays all our focus to unfold his seminar onto anxiety and the object *a*, the rift where the rescuing of castration from the complex takes place, and where the pervert is given—for the first time in the history of psychoanalysis—the position of the witness of the neurotic's *deception*. Only perversion can indicate by its truthfulness in wanting a phallus that what neurosis is after (in the phallus) is its lack, that the phallus for neurosis is but a bluff. One mustn't dismiss the extensive and diverse references Lacan makes to perversion at every major moment of Seminar X. Perversion becomes so essential to him in explaining neurosis that he is left with no other choice than trusting the pervert. The first of those references appears right before Lacan uncovers *Heim*, to address this rift between neurosis and perversion in the most systematic manner there can be:

> For the pervert, things are, if I may say so, in their right place. The a is right where the subject can't see it and the capital S is in its place. This is why one can say that the perverse subject, whilst remaining oblivious to the way this functions, offers himself loyally to the Other's jouissance.
>
> Only, we'd never have known anything about it had it not been for the neurotics, for whom the fantasy doesn't possess at all the same functioning. The neurotic is the one who reveals the fantasy in its structure because of what he makes of it, but also, at the same time, through what he makes of it, he cons you, like he cons everyone. (Lacan 2014, 49)

Is it the neurotic's conning that reveals to us the pervert's fantasy—to "offer himself loyally to the Other's jouissance"—as Lacan tells us here, or is it the other way around? Hasn't the neurotic conned us enough since Freud by convincing us there was a thing they were after, until this moment where Lacan introduces them again to us, accompanied by their "loyal" double, the pervert? Why does Lacan give us the reversed order of his reasoning here if not to give the pervert sufficient status to reveal back, in the neurotic, what they have not—*Heim*? The proof comes right afterward: "Neurotics have perverse fantasies and analysts have been racking their brains for a good while wondering what this means. At any rate, one can very well see that it's not the same thing as perversion, that it doesn't function in the same way, and a whole mix-up is produced, and questions mount up, and people wonder for example whether a perversion is really a perversion, in other words whether perchance it might not be functioning as does the fantasy for the neurotic. This question merely duplicates the first one of what use is the perverse fantasy to the neurotic?" (Lacan 2014, 50).

Things are in their right order now, Lacan questions neurosis by perversion and prepares the extraction. The neurotic's use of fantasy (i.e., the pervert's fantasy of the Oedipus complex), as opposed to the pervert's, comprises the failure of this very fantasy, a failure whose function is to preserve a lack in the Other:

> It's striking that the fantasy the neurotic makes use of, which he organizes at the very moment he uses it, is precisely what serves him best in defending himself against anxiety, in keeping a lid on it. [...] This object a that the neurotic makes himself into in his fantasy becomes him much like gaiters do a rabbit. That's why the neurotic never makes much of his fantasy [as opposed to the pervert]. It succeeds in defending him against anxiety precisely to the extent that it's a postiche a. I illustrated this function for you a long while ago with the dream dreamt by the butcher's beautiful wife. (Lacan 1962–1963/1981, 50)

What does Lacan tell us here other than that neurosis is *a perversion of perversion?* For where the pervert offers themself as the Other's unmistakable object, which they make much of in terms of the Other's jouissance, the neurotic doesn't offer more than a *postiche a*—that is, a deception they use as a lid to cover their anxiety. The whole point for the neurotic is to keep their jouissance out of the Other, to keep the Other lacking it by making sure that he desires it in them without ever getting it; but all that, on the basis of believing that the Other has it, that the Other is one, which is the source of the neurotic's anxiety. What Lacan shows us, here, is the only clinical entry point into an undeceived concept of neurosis. For the cutting edge that distinguishes the neurotic from the pervert, at the moment where the Other has taken this *postiche a* to be real—when the Other has been *deceived*, when the Other enjoys, when he doesn't lack anything—is anxiety. For Lacan shows us later on how this function of anxiety fails in perversion (Lacan 2014, 165). This is where it becomes clear for us that what the neurotic was after in the first place was no phallus at all.

This reversal of the classical conception of neurosis—which placed it for a long while in position of the first criterion, inasmuch as perversion was conceived as being a perversion of neurosis—certainly scrambles theoretical aspirations in the linearity of psychic development, which have always ended in a rebranding of normality. Nevertheless, one must admit that in the classical tentative of defining perversion as standing in the realm of the unresolvable Oedipal complex, and thereby prior to neurosis in terms of evolution, there was a course correction (although a failed one) that contains some truth—neurosis is extractable from perversion. The whole neurotic enterprise is one step further from the complex, at the very breaking point with its logic, that is the necessity of the Other's lack. For if there is a thing to which the neurotic's turmoil can be reduced, it precisely is how not to allow this identification of the Oedipus complex to become complete, for that has only one name, the *Unheimliche* (the uncanny).

Allow me now to introduce *Heim*, before concluding this induction, as inscribed—already—in the dialectic of the drive. For although Lacan's final revision of the drive stands a long way from this extraction I have investigated, there is something that makes it an immediate conceptual necessity. One simply cannot approach the *Heimliche* and the *Unheimliche* apart from alienation and separation, for they are one and the same thing. "The Unheimliche is defined as Heimliche. The Unheim is poised in the

Heim" (Lacan 2014, 47). So anxiety is the signal of that *Heim*—that is lack, the subject's lacked jouissance—has become an *Unheim*, that it has become the Other's, that *Heim* has gotten estranged or alienated. "Man finds his home at a point located in the Other that lies beyond the image from which we are fashioned. This place represents the absence where we stand. […] This place is tantamount to an absence" (Lacan 2014, 47).

Heim, in other words, is the Other's lacked jouissance which guarantees that the subject's alienation to the signifier is incomplete and that separation is still possible—that there still is a *remainder* of jouissance out of the Other to cause desire. And anxiety is the signal that separation is no longer possible, hence uncanniness. Therefore, where the neurotic reveal themself as a "*postiche a*," what they intend is to keep the Other desiring, and thereby lacking—they sustain their *Heim* by the Other's desire (Lacan 2014, 50). "The true object sought out by the neurotic [as opposed to the pervert] is a demand that he wants to be asked of him," they demand nothing else than the Other's lack (Lacan 2014, 51). This is where the extrapolation of demand and anxiety departs from, to reach formalization in *that which deceives* and *that which deceives not.*

Kierkegaard, from Affect to Subjectivation

In this section, I follow Lacan's path in Seminar X from "that which deceives" (i.e., the signifier) all the way up to "anxiety between jouissance and desire," that is the function of anxiety in subjectivation. This will demand a thorough reading of Kierkegaard's *Concept of Anxiety*, from which Lacan deduces the function of affect and the concept of object *a*, and on the basis of which he formulates the three stages of subjectivation. Let us pick up Lacan's argument from the distinction between the sign and the signifier; the signifier's course—as opposed to the sign's—aims always back at the subject from which it departs (Lacan 2014, 62). After showing the abundant usage of traces by animal species, Lacan comes to the radical factor that opposes the speaking subject to other species—that is, their turning of the trace into a signifier. "There's one thing that animals don't do—they don't lay false traces to make us believe that they are false. […] When a trace has been made to be taken for a false trace […]

we know that there's a speaking subject, we know that there's a subject as cause" (Lacan 2014, 63).

This laying of a false trace, whose very laying makes sure to denote as being false, precludes a bet on the "Other's rationality," on the one hand, and on the other hand, dooms this rational Other to not knowing anything about this—now signifying—trace, other than that there is an empty place—a subject—that causes it (Lacan 2014, 63). We must highlight already how the subject, in Lacan's procedure, doesn't come to the forefront without the notion of *cause*. Further, its body is a gap—a lack—in signification. There is a subject only when there is a cause, and there is a cause only when there is a gap—something that signification cannot grasp (*Heim*). "The cause always comes to the surface in correlation with the fact that something is omitted in cognition's consideration. [...] Each time the cause is brought up, and in its most traditional register, the cause is the shadow, or the counterpart, of what stands as a blind spot in the function of cognizance" (Lacan 2014, 217).

This should remind us of the obsessive, for instance, who—unlike the hysteric—displays this in pure form. For if there is a word that could name such a discursive art as the obsessive's, which is mostly silence, it is the ungraspable. They speak, one may say, in favor of pure cause, as pure as it takes for them to be the Other's guarantor—the ultimate subject. That is why Lacan alludes further in the seminar to how the obsessive's analysis may be considered as ended when their transference neurosis "is fully present."

To return to Lacan's procedure, he equates this functioning of the false trace with that of demand, which is always held by signifiers, telling us that when demand is given a response that fills it, when demand is taken for a true trace, when the *postiche a* is taken for a real, demand loses what it sustains—through fallacy—of its cause (Lacan 2014, 64). Demand loses what it sustains of the subject by lack (*Heim*), the subject then has to respond by that which deceives not: anxiety. And this is a point one may find elucidated anywhere in the hysteric's romantic tragedies, at the moment when getting loved with such a passion as that which was fantasized turns out to be a curse. A curse that is, often, not a slighter curse than the one there is in not being loved at all. For the lack of lack is on both ends; extreme passion to the extent of captivity and no passion at all are both equal indications that the hysteric is not being lacked, that the Other lacks him or her not, and therefore that jouissance is in the Other. He is either enjoying him or her or enjoying without him or her; the bottom line is that he's enjoying—"what am I, then?"

After this introduction, Lacan tells us that "the first thing to put forward concerning the structure of anxiety [...] is that anxiety is framed" (Lacan 2014, 73). For insofar as the sign's function—as opposed to the signifier's—is to point out something for someone, and insofar as this pointing comes to counter the signifier's deception, anxiety acts as a frame. For what is pointing out something for someone, after all, other than framing it for him to see? This is where Lacan compares anxiety and its framing to a stage, whose function in a play is to ensure the presence of another world in the world, whereby the tragicomic dimension emerges. This tragicomic dimension, he tells us, is "that which may not be said," for saying is deceiving insomuch as, in saying, the subject of enunciation becomes the subject of the enounced (Lacan 2014, 75). And from that point, he chooses to take on the path of temporality to introduce the pivotal articulation he borrows from Kierkegaard. "Without this introductive moment of anxiety, which quickly dies away, nothing would be able to take on its value of what will be determined thereafter as tragic or comic" (Lacan 2014, 75).

What Lacan advances through this temporality—anxiety as introductive moment—is Kierkegaard's "pre-sentiment" (Kierkegaard 1957, 55). Anxiety is "that which stands prior to the first appearance of a feeling," whose true weight is "keeping up the function of cause" (Lacan 2014, 75). The feeling or sentiment, we must remember, is one step further than anxiety into intelligibility; for one may identify a feeling, a feeling may be spoken and spoken about, and this is why there is a multitude of feelings that have different names—they were symbolically distinguished one from the other. Fear, for instance, is a feeling; but it is not the case for anxiety. There isn't but one anxiety, which provides sufficient evidence on it being ungraspable and unspeakable. This is where Lacan calls upon Kierkegaard's "pre-sentiment," to situate anxiety as prior to sentiment, on the one hand, and as opposed to it, on the other hand—inasmuch as anxiety, unlike sentiment, produces a gap in signification (a silence) that sentiment (or feeling), left to itself, would fill with speech. And this is the *gap* in signification—the lack in the Other—in line with which Lacan assigns to anxiety the task of "keeping up the function of cause."

When Lacan speaks of cause, however, he is by no means referring to anything of the kind of the stability of the order of *reason*. He doesn't even use causality as it functions in Kant's *Transcendental Aesthetics*; rather, he extracts a notion of causality from Kant's use of the term "gap" to describe the cause's analytic irreducibility (Lacan 2014, 282). And where this extraction is sufficiently explained is not in Seminar X but in Seminar XI.

> Some of you at least will remain unsatisfied if I simply point out that, in his "An attempt to introduce the concept of negative quantities into philosophy," we can see how closely Kant comes to understanding the gap that the function of cause has always presented to any conceptual apprehension. In that essay, it is more or less stated that cause is a concept that, in the last resort, is unanalyzable—impossible to understand by reason—if indeed the rule of reason, the Venunftsregel is always some Vergleichung, or equivalent—and that there remains essentially in the function of cause a certain gap, a term used by Kant in the Prolegomena. (Lacan 1981, 21)

In other words, if the irreducible of a causal relation is indeed its necessary resort to comparison (for cause is cause on the basis of a rule deduced from comparison), then the cause by which the whole movement of reason gets enabled is a gap in reason itself—that is, its encounter with negativity (Lacan 1981, 21). This particular engagement with the gap in causality is not to be addressed as a simple resourcing that Lacan finds in Transcendental Aesthetics to inscribe the subject of the unconscious; it is rather a venture that aims at reinscribing reason itself in its relation to truth—as it departs from the encounter of thinking with the real. This thus affirms that the subject of the unconscious is none other than that of reason, if not that they are one and the same. I return to this idea in the following section of this chapter where I discuss *The Subversion of the Subject* to extract Lacan's answer to the question of the Other's ontological status.

Now though let us turn to Lacan's reference to Kierkegaard before moving any further in the function of anxiety and the formalization of the three stages of subjectivation; for it is to Kierkegaard that we owe this linkage of anxiety to the function of cause in the first place, and thus also its placement between jouissance and desire. Let us pick up Kierkeggard's argument from where he disagrees with (the Danish transmission of) Hegel on innocence as being the immediate—that is, that which "needs to be annulled" (Kierkegaard 1957, 32). Kierkegaard underlines that innocence—inasmuch as it is only a retrospection from the outset of guilt—cannot be annulled, for innocence "only comes into existence by the very fact that it is annulled" (Kierkegaard 1957, 32–33). He reaffirms, in this way, the Hegelian position, beyond its mistaken transmission, that immediacy is part of mediacy, and moves on to deduce that what is posed in innocence—insofar as immediacy cannot precede mediacy, being its result—is simply the absence of the henceforth established knowledge; therefore, that "innocence is ignorance" (Kierkegaard 1957, 33–34). This brings Kierkegaard to the fundamental problem of desire, for if innocence occurs as lost only by the establishment of knowledge, then how did Adam, the first of men, lose his ignorance (Kierkegaard 1957, 34)? How has he gotten into knowledge out of a prohibition?

On that, Kierkegaard challenges Usteri's answer which proposes that if prohibition has been sufficient for the establishment of sin, then prohibition itself is knowledge on the possibility of sin and is therefore commandment of desire (Kierkegaard 1957, 36). What Kierkegaard claims in response is that, although what is desired is always in relation to the prohibited, one cannot postulate that *concupiscentia* logically succeeds prohibition, provided that concupiscentia determines guilt and sin as much as it is determined by them. In other words, concupiscentia must precede prohibition as much as it succeeds it, and therefore, "the fall [of Adam in sin] becomes something progressive" (Kierkegaard 1957, 37). And from that point, which reattributes to the origin of concupiscentia its full ambiguity—by dismissing its reduction by Usteri to an effect of prohibition, that is, to pure ethical foundations—Kierkegaard calls forth his concept of objective anxiety. As Kierkegaard writes, "Innocence is ignorance. [...] In this state there is peace and, repose: but at the same time there is something different, which is not dissension and strife, for there is nothing to strive with. What is it then? Nothing. What effect does nothing produce? It begets dread. This is the profound secret of innocence, that at the same time it is dread. Dream. Singly the spirit projects its own reality, but this reality is nothing, but this nothing constantly sees innocence outside of it" (Kierkegaard 1957, 37).

In other words, what in innocence is irreducible to innocence—innocence being innocence only from the outset of knowledge—is *nothing*, it is lack as state. But why is it anxiety that *nothing* generates to project itself as irreducible real? Anxiety, Kierkegaard tells us, is the only "form which entices its possibility," provided that anxiety is "no more than a signal"—for more than a signal is bound to reintroduce this *nothing* within the realm of the ethical, and thus in the mediacy of the knowledge that bars its possibility. "The reality of the spirit constantly shows itself in a form which entices its possibility, but it is away as soon as one grasps after it, and it is a nothing which is able only to alarm. More it cannot do so long as it only shows itself" (Kierkegaard 1957, 38).

Kierkegaard advances, therefore, two formal propositions defining the function of anxiety. The first proposition is "dread is freedom's reality as possibility of possibility," that he introduces in opposition to fear "which refers to something definite" (Kierkegaard 1957, 38). What Kierkegaard tells us anxiety's object to be, here, as opposed to the object of fear, is a negative object—a pure possibility, a lack which he illustrates later on in anxiety as a "seeking after adventure, a thirst for the prodigious, the mysterious" (Kierkegaard 1957, 38). The second proposition is "dread is a sympathetic antipathy and an antipathetic sympathy," whereby he underlines the state of tension that anxiety sustains—comprising as much attraction as repulsion—with its object, and that, for its object to be kept in the realm of possibility—that is lack as such or *nothing* (Kierkegaard 1957, 38–39). In other words, for *nothing* to remain *nothing*, it must be repulsed as much as it attracts.

Kierkegaard returns, then, with those two propositions in hand and opposes the sufficiency of prohibition in inscribing desire in man. He also opposes by the same token the validity of original sin; for desire, insofar as it departs from anxiety, remains desire for *nothing*, it is therefore no sinful choice that is made in response to prohibition. "He who through dread becomes guilty is innocent," Kierkegaard explains, for he has desired—that is to say dreaded—lack as such. Kierkegaard advances from this point onto that giving such a validity to the original sin (in concupiscentia) undermines the very presence of spirit that he equates with the subject, which he calls forth, now, in position of synthesis between the soulish and the bodily (Kierkegaard 1957, 38–39). This synthesis where spirit is to be ascribed, he tells us, is impossible by other means than a relation, a relation of spirit to itself—which entails its becoming for itself—and a relation that is necessarily anxiety.

> How is spirit related to itself and to its situation? It is related as dread. The spirit cannot do away with itself; nor can it grasp itself so long as it has itself outside of itself. Neither can man sink down into the vegetative life, for he is determined as spirit. He cannot flee from dread, for he loves it; really he does not love it, for he flees from it. Innocence has now reached its apex. It is ignorance, but not an animal brutality, but an ignorance which is qualified by spirit, but which precisely is dread, because its ignorance is about nothing. Here there is no knowledge of good and evil, etc., but the whole reality of knowledge is projected in dread as the immense nothing of ignorance. (Kierkegaard 1957, 40)

In other words, provided that spirit is not in itself, it is bound to realize itself for itself, which can occur neither by the medium of the ethical nor by that of the ontological—for it loses itself as much in trying to grasp itself "as outside of itself" (i.e., as ethical) as in "sinking down into the vegetative life" (i.e., as ontological). Therefore, spirit's only relation to itself whereby it becomes for itself is anxiety, which forms the medium that allows it to project its possibility—that is ignorance or *nothing*—in knowledge. In other words, what Kierkegaard advances here is that, inasmuch as in anxiety spirit becomes for itself, the knowledge in which it is projected is not knowledge but the possibility of ignorance—a crucial point we will return to. In that, we reach the climax of Kierkegaard's venture, for at the point of revealing to us spirit's relation to itself whereby it becomes for itself, he reminds us that spirit can neither be ethical nor be ontological, nor can it "do away with itself" either. In other words, that both the ethical and the ontological lack the real and are thus incomplete; that nature and culture are incomplete, and that the gap between them—that is the incompleteness of both—is the "nothing of ignorance" that is spirit. On that, one may hint already at why Lacan categorizes this gap in

Seminar XI as being "pre-ontological," for this is the very reasoning wherefrom subjectivation appears to necessitate a further reaching retroaction than ontology, which Lacan formalizes in the object being an *object cause* (Lacan 1981, 29).

Yet, although we have seen already how Kierkegaard gives Lacan every reason to formalize the nothing of spirit as a negative object, the subject as a retroaction from ethical to pre-ontological as withheld in the function of cause, and anxiety's unsignifierability as affect, we may want to address two additional ideas he advances further in the essay, for Kierkegaard has been a little more generous to Lacan than we might think. The first is a deduction that steps so close to that the first signifier is a naming whereby the real is negativized (which I address in detail in the following section of this chapter) and the second is that *anxiety precedes desire*—wherefrom descend the *three stages of subjectivation.*

Let us start with the first point. In his further speculations, Kierkegaard writes that if God did voice out prohibition to Adam, that would suppose that Adam could utter it—and thus that Adam had knowledge prior to prohibition, therefore, that he was not innocent. He deduces from this that it couldn't have been God that voiced out the prohibition, or any spirit that is supposed to know, but must have been Adam himself (Kierkegaard 1957, 41). Kierkegaard deduces from this that language could already speak in Adam, well before the establishment of knowledge, without him being able to utter it (Kierkegaard 1957, 41). And he supports this idea—a little further in the page—with the biblical statement that God had given Adam the ability to name things prior to prohibition (Kierkegaard 1957, 41). Consequently, what occurs at the moment where prohibition is voiced out in him, his first uttering of this prohibition, Kierkegaard tells us, right before the retroactive establishment of knowledge from its outset, is necessarily "only intelligible to freedom," that is to say is only uttered in the terms of the *possibility of possibility* that anxiety had already established in its *projection* of nothing prior to prohibition (Kierkegaard 1957, 41). "Innocence can very well utter this distinction [freedom, possibility of possibility], but the distinction is not for it, and for it this has only the significance we have shown above [nothing]" (Kierkegaard 1957, 41). In other words, the first word Adam grasps as prohibition and turns into signifier is necessarily the name of his pure possibility—that is negativity—which, by the fact of getting named (as freedom), is negativized. This is precisely what Kierkegaard formalizes out of the idea (he advances earlier) that, as far as spirit is concerned, knowledge stands for the possibility of ignorance—or nothing. Kierkegaard writes a whole section afterward, not without provoking his fellow contemporaries, on the structural lack of knowledge—which one wouldn't encounter again before Durkheim and Mauss's works on *mana*, that Lacan's debate with Lévi-Strauss on the nature of S1 will lead to an end (Kierkegaard 1957, 46). We will see in the next section that this is the point where the end of structuralism is announced, and with it the errancy of the analytic praxis, but let us retain for now that Kierkegaard has gotten to S1 because he managed to depart from the Hegelian grounds that anxiety precedes sin and desire and that Lacan proceeds in the same manner in Seminar X, which allows him to rescue castration from complex.

The second and last remark I would like to underline, before returning to Lacan, appears as soon as Kierkegaard draws a line between the objective dread—that precedes sin—and the subjective dread—that succeeds it (Kierkegaard 1957, 49). Objective dread is "the dread felt by innocence, which is the reflex of freedom within itself at the thought of its possibility," and subjective dread "is the dread posited in the individual as the consequence of his sin" (Kierkegaard 1957, 51). One needn't point out here that these are not two separate dreads but two functions of dread, before and after subjectivation—that is, the alienation that occurs together with the subject's entry into the world of the signifier by the medium of S1. So what does dread become after one's subjection to the first signifier? Kierkegaard answers this question in the following terms: "Dread [subjective dread] is [...] the most egoistic thing, and no concrete expression of freedom is so egoistic as is the possibility of every concretion. This again is the overwhelming experience which determines the individual's ambiguous relation, both sympathetic and antipathetic. In dread there is the egoistic infinity of possibility, which does not tempt like a definite choice, but alarms (angster) and fascinates with its sweet anxiety (*Be-ængstelse*)" (Kierkegaard 1957, 55).

One must question the term *again*, here—"this again is the overwhelming experience which determines the individual's ambiguous relation, both sympathetic and antipathetic." Is that an "again" whereby Kierkegaard defines dread "again" with the "sympathetic and antipathetic" he used already for objective dread? Or is it an "again" pertaining to the idea that subjective dread aims at returning "again" to its primordial form—objective dread—to counter spirit's *alienation* to the signifier? The rest of the quote may answer the question quite efficiently. "Subjective dread is the most egoistic thing, and no concrete expression of freedom is so egoistic as is the possibility of every concretion." Any "concrete expression of freedom" and "every concretion" are clear references to signification; no signification is ever enough, Kierkegaard tells us, to withhold the spirit's freedom (i.e., *nothing*); for that, it must annul them all by subjective dread to return "again" to "the egoistic infinity of possibility, which does not temp like a definite choice, but alarms and fascinates with its sweet anxiety." In other words, anxiety after subjectivation is objection to subjectivation, a tentative of returning to a state prior to signification—subjective dread is therefore separation—that is to be addressed as distinct from guilt (Kierkegaard 1957, 55). Kierkegaard writes: "Here then the nothing of dread is a complex of presentiments which reflect themselves in themselves, coming nearer and nearer to the individual, notwithstanding that in dread they signify again essentially nothing, not, however, be it noted, a nothing with which the individual has nothing to do, but a nothing in lively communication with the ignorance of innocence" (Kierkegaard 1957, 55). The self-referentiality of anxiety—"presentiments which reflect themselves in themselves"—is clearly posed, here, in opposition to signification—"in dread they signify essentially nothing." What does not signify addresses itself to itself. Yet this *nothing* opposing signification is not "a nothing with which the individual has nothing to do," Kierkegaard tells us, it isn't an unintended *nothing*—as in the "animal brutality"—but "a nothing in lively communication with the ignorance of innocence"; it is Adam hearing his possibility "again" in a name, as it were in his initial subjectivation, which has only one possible outcome, that is, the production of a new S1—it is entering language and sin anew, whereby both get modified in repetition. Without stepping into the business of whether that makes any sin ever enough—which renders original sin rather the one ever to come than the first to have occurred—let us leave Kierkegaard's reasoning to turn to the formalization Lacan will draw out of it.

The central point Kierkegaard's venture unfolds out of is the Hegelian postulate that pure or immediate being, or *nothing*, constitutes the origin of the dialectic of subjectivation—although it is made clear in Hegel that this origin is only made possible to posit retroactively. As Kierkegaard writes, "Innocence is ignorance. [...] In this state there is peace and, repose: but at the same time there is something different, which is not dissension and strife, for there is nothing to strive with. What is it then? Nothing. What effect does nothing produce? It begets dread" (Kierkegaard 1957, 37). This axiom must be very dear to us, for Lacan will not only place it at the heart of his final formalization—"this etwas [something], faced with which anxiety operates as a signal, belongs to the realm of the real's irreducibility"—but will also assign to this formalization the task of realigning it with Hegel's retroaction (Lacan 2014, 160). And that, insofar as he posits anxiety to beget desire as in Kierkegaard, yet, to be begotten not by nothing—for this nothing only becomes nothing by S1—but by what originally is the incompleteness of jouissance (the drive) which propels toward nothing. So where Lacan says "anxiety between jouissance and desire," he does nothing less than reverse Kierkegaard's postulate from "nothing begets dread" to "dread begets nothing." And this reversal is not without foundations, for there is in it the inscription of Kierkegaard's subjectivation within the condition of the notion of surplus. In other words, Lacan reworks this axiom in light of the fact that nothing—being the surplus—only becomes nothing by its extrapolation from itself (in its doubling) as pure possibility of itself—that is to say that nothing is not in itself but only becomes nothing for itself. What Lacan introduces is that, although jouissance tends to nothing for jouissance is negation, it is not nothing, it is all but nothing; that jouissance is that for which no nothing (as negation) is ever enough, and whose tragedy, therefore, is precisely in that it can never become nothing—it can never die in satisfaction. In Dolar's words, "it is a drive which itself cannot die. It is a pure thrust of persistence which cannot be annihilated, it can merely be destroyed from outside, a pure life in the loop of death, emerging on the verge of nothing" (Dolar 2005, 159). There is no point, therefore, where being advances itself as a nothing that precedes affect (which is not nothing),

nothing only becomes itself by a retroaction from affect. For where Kierkegaard leads us with the idea that Adam couldn't have uttered in the first signifier of prohibition other than his possibility—that is nothing—is that this possibility was already, and since the very start, out of his reach, in objective dread. Why would he have seen nothing in sin otherwise if this nothing was already at hand? Why would he have adhered to prohibition by desire if it did not withhold for him something more—*nothing*—than what he already was, in the midst of all that freedom of his objective dread? The most elementary deduction that one derives from Kierkegaard's reasoning, therefore, is that, in anxiety, Adam had been burning—a point Kierkegaard is clear on where he tells us that Adam couldn't love dread without fleeing it, and that in this burning this nothing was already not nothing (Kierkegaard 1957, 40). This is the logical necessity there is for nothing to be found, at last, as possibility of possibility in the signifier of prohibition. It is only from this amendment, now, that one may grasp Kierkegaard's ingenious doubling of possibility in his formula—"the possibility of possibility"—beyond the elucidation of a pure potentiality. Why would Kierkegaard multiply this possibility by itself if not to signify that, by this doubling, possibility has in fact gotten barred, that it has precisely become a possibility by getting asserted as impossibility? One may deduce, thus, that jouissance appears as possibility of possibility—and thus nothing—the very instant that Adam is divided from it by prohibition and desire—which is what Hegel advances in the idea that self-equality does not precede the dialectic, but comes into play as its result, that is, as estrangement. And one needn't speculate on such a tragedy as that of genesis to reach such a deduction, for the psychotic is there to testify; jouissance as such is all but nothing; even more, if it were anything, it would be nothing's very foreclosure.

To return to Lacan's argument now, nothing—that is, the Other's lack (i.e., desire) as object *a*—is the remainder of jouissance at the point of the subject's alienation to the signifier. Only then does jouissance become its possibility (i.e., nothing). This is the amendment whereby Lacan reorganizes Kierkegaard's subjectivation in three stages:

> The a is what remains of the irreducible [jouissance] in the complete operation of the subject's advent in the locus of the Other and it is from this that

> it will derive its function. [...] This is what we are dealing with, on one hand in desire, on the other in anxiety. In anxiety, we are dealing with it at a moment that logically precedes the moment at which we deal with it in desire. [...] To connote the three stages of the operation of division, we shall say that here at the start there is an x that we can only name retroactively, which is properly speaking the inroad to the Other, the essential target at which the subject has to place himself. Here we have the level of anxiety, constitutive of the appearance of the function. And it is with the third term that the $ appears as subject of desire. (Lacan 2014, 161)

So, first stage, Adam is an "x that we can only name retroactively"; this is jouissance as such that the infant experiences in the real Other's response, and it is "the inroad to the Other" inasmuch as this jouissance forms the springboard to the infant's call—the cry—which the Other will interpret as demand and will respond to from the outset of his desire. Second stage, "we have the level of anxiety, constitutive of the appearance of the *a* function"; this is Adam's objective dread that projects jouissance as possibility in *a*—nothing—by the medium of S1. It is the remainder there is between jouissance as such in (x) and the Other's response to the infant's call, which implies an insignia of the Other's desire. And third stage, "the $ appears as subject of desire"; Adam becomes the subject of the desire caused by his possibility in the *a*—nothing—and is split from himself as jouissance by its possibility—that is, its impossibility.

All the deductions on desire one finds dispersed in Seminar X derive from this order of subjectivation. To conclude this section, allow me to briefly list these deductions in six points—which I articulate in the following section of the chapter.

(1) Anxiety precedes desire (i.e., castration) and therefore anxiety is not a castration anxiety; it is rather an alienation anxiety insofar as it signals that the lost jouissance has become the Other's, that the Other is one (Lacan 2014, 53). And we owe this to Kierkegaard, not to Lacan, for he is the one to uncover that objective dread precedes sin (i.e., desire) and that subjective dread aims at desubjectivation beyond guilt.
(2) Provided that desire's function is to sustain jouissance as possibility (*nothing* or *a*), desire and castration are one, for to desire is to abide

by the law of language that prohibits jouissance as such; and it is only in that that jouissance becomes its possibility (Lacan 1962–1963, 1981, 106).

(3) Inasmuch as desire is the path of the law, desire leads to no more than inciting desire, desire is but a loop, and satisfaction—as it occurs in a falling out of the object at the anxiety-point—is rather a disruption to desire than a logical outcome (Lacan 2014, 231).

(4) Provided that satisfaction reveals the object as being missed in its image, for its occurrence is tied to the fall of the object into its lack *(a)*, the object is not an *object of desire* but an *object cause of desire* (Lacan 2014, 175).

(5) Inasmuch as the object is an object lack (the Other's lack, that is, the Other's desire in S1), castration, beyond its imaginary function as complex, is no longer the lack of the object, but the object itself—that is, the Other's castration. And the phallus which positivizes it by the complex, on the other end, operates as the sign (of the missing jouissance) whereby jouissance gets restituted to the Other as an ever-missing signifier—the signifier yet to come (Lacan 2014, 46).

(6) Provided that the object lack is the remainder of jouissance—that is, the subject prior to subjectivation *(x)*—the object represents the subject themself as remainder of their own division. The conceptual division of object and subject falls, therefore, and that is why Lacan calls the object by a nonsignifying letter *a* (Lacan 2014, 86).

We shall see in the following section how those six points are not only the theoretical deductions that lay the foundations of our praxis but also the ones that constitute the endpoint to our experience. That is to say that any analysand who has gone all the way till the end of the riddle of their desire, regardless of how well informed they are of those axioms, has had them already engraved by experience on experience itself.

The Possible Encounter

Let us depart again from where Kierkegaard led us (in the previous section), which is that nature and culture are both incomplete, and that spirit (*nothing*) is the incompleteness of both at once; which makes of nothing a double nothing, for there is the incompleteness of nature on one hand (the gap in the bodily) and the incompleteness of culture on the other (the gap in the soul). If one goes back to Lacan's amendment now (i.e., the schema where he substitutes jouissance to Kierkegaard's nothing in the first stage of subjectivation and calls it (*x*), and displaces this *nothing* then into the second or middle stage and calls it (*a*)), one would figure out that the most direct outcome of this amendment is that nothing is no longer the gap in nature and culture but the *gap* between them; the *a* becomes a gap between jouissance and the Other (Lacan 2014, 162). And although this idea of in between was already alluded to by Kierkegaard—for he advances spirit as synthesis of body and soul—Lacan's amendment brings into the equation an additional character: nothing is no longer the synthetic gap between nature and culture; it is rather the gap wherein each at the point of its own ontological lack calls forth its opposite to sustain its subjectivation. So, (1) nature and culture are incomplete, (2) their incompleteness is a gap between them, (3) this gap is therefore double, and (4) those two facets of the gap are the symbolic's reducibility to the real and the real's reducibility to the symbolic, at the point of each's ontological lack.

To put things in clinically tangible terms, this doubling of lack is that which makes, simultaneously, no jouissance ever enjoyable or sufficient and no symbolization ever complete; inasmuch as each ends up revealing that the irreducible atom of its constitution lies in its opposite. And this is a proposition to which psychosis and perversion form the most radical of oppositions. For the psychotic's wager, for instance, is in a complete and self-propelled jouissance to be found in some ultimate freedom from the Other; although they are constantly caught by the fact that the more jouissance is freed from this Other the more it becomes his. As for the pervert, it is the wager that the symbolic is sufficient and worthy of the ultimate sacrifice of jouissance; yet, insofar as the pervert appoint themself the guardian of this sacrifice, it is as Other that they enjoy it. The neurotic, however, with their S1 and their castration complex in hand, have the double wager of exchanging jouissance's incompleteness with its possibility in the Other's completeness, and of reverting back this exchange by posing themself as the jouissance the Other lacks—anxiety. In short, setting out from Hegelian grounds allows one to address neurosis—as the foundational problem of psychoanalysis—as the dialectical condition whereby incompleteness on one side of the equation implicates completeness on the other; the condition whereby lack on one side is positivized on the other. *New-rosis*—to spell it correctly—means that the incompleteness of jouissance and the incompleteness of the Other cannot meet, and there gets laid the necessity of the new, regardless of whether it is the new that desire brings (alienation), or the one that brings desire (separation). *New-rosis* is the necessity of the new, which, in turn, is repetition—that is, the cyclical alternation of the positivization of lack between symbolic and real.

The question of analysis becomes, thus, as far as the neurotic is concerned, how to make those two lacks encounter each other, how to make them dissociate one from the other—the lack of jouissance in the Other as a fact of S1 and the lack of jouissance itself as a fact of its immediacy. This is the problem to be tackled by any true ambition of affecting—in the only possible encounter that the dialectic permits—the castration complex that positivizes the lack in jouissance in the Other's completeness, rendering jouissance thereby complete. To address this problem satisfyingly, we are required to follow the whole questioning of the Other's ontology that stretches from Emile Durkheim's excavation of mana to the works of Marcel Mauss and the formalizations Claud Lévi-Strauss drew out of them before arriving at Lacan's inaugural answer on those formalizations—where the incompleteness of the Other becomes the theoretical springboard for addressing the incompleteness of jouissance. For any prospect of arriving at a concept of an end to analysis requires that we follow the path of this theoretical engagement that Lacan affords in *The Subversion of the Subject.*

Let us depart from Durkheim's extraction of the first outlines of the notion of mana, wherefrom our apprehension of the incompleteness of the symbolic becomes possible. Mana is a Melanesian signifier who's first uncovering by Codrington is revisited and formalized by Durkheim in *Elementary Forms of Religious Life* as that which "involves the very idea of sacredness itself" (Durkheim 1915, 186). It represents "an anonymous and defused force [...] located nowhere definitely and it is everywhere," a force that is marked by a complete impersonality. Yet, despite this impersonality whereby mana insures its omnipresence, Durkheim places it at the core of the totemic principle wherein the making of a divinity represents it in a "specialized form" (Durkheim 1915, 194–95). As to the phenomena that "mana" names, he tells us with astonishing precision, "magic forces are thought of as being all of the same nature; the mind represents them in their generic unity" (Durkheim 1915, 198). In other words, what "mana" names is all possibilities of the unknown as one, it is a category of its own, and a category that has no opposite—for its opposite is all other signifiers within its structure, that is, all what knowledge may cover (Durkheim 1915, 198). "It is owing to his mana that a man succeeds in hunting or fighting, that gardens give a good return or that flocks prosper. If an arrow strikes its mark, it is because it is charged with mana; it is the same cause which makes a net catch fish well, or a canoe ride well on the sea, etc. It is true that if certain phrases of Codrington are taken literally, mana should be the cause to which is attributed 'everything which is beyond the ordinary power of men, outside the common processes of nature'" (Durkheim 1915, 204). What one finds in those lines is a crucial addition on the nature of the phenomena that *mana* names, for what Durkheim tells us here is that it is not the simple unknown but that which of the unknown ensures a causal function at the point of cognizance's encounter with the real. Mana, in other words, is the *cause* wherever it presents itself in its true form, that is a gap in cognizance. "The concept of mana," he adds, "is applied only to those [events] that are important enough to cause reflection, and to awaken a minimum of interest and curiosity" (Durkheim 1915, 204).

Let us add to that one more line from Durkheim's extraction—that we shall place in direct sequence with the notion of *cause*—which assigns to mana the most elementary outline of subjectivity: "The idea of mana does not presuppose the idea of the soul for if the mana is going to individualize itself and break itself up into the particular souls, it must first of all exist, and what it is in itself does not depend upon the forms it takes when individualized. But on the contrary, the idea of the soul cannot be understood except when taken in connection with the idea of mana" (Durkheim 1915, 267). What Durkheim tells us here is, first, that mana represents a negativity given that it is indivisible—for its division requires that it positively exists—and unaffectable by "the forms it takes when individualized" and, second, that the idea of the soul is inconceivable other than through its foundation in this negativity (cause, gap) that mana insures in signification.

If we turn our attention now to where Marcel Mauss takes up the task of addressing the function of mana as a form of knowledge in *A General Theory of Magic*, besides the multiple uses he makes of it elsewhere (object of exchange, foundation of value and symbolic debt, honor and authority), we'd find him arriving at a common category (by way of identifying mana as the foundation of magic) that unites all the contradictory semantic unfoldings of mana, a category he calls "power-milieu" (Mauss 1923–1924, 156, 2001, 138).

> At the same time as being a material substance, which can be localized, it is also spiritual. It works at a distance and also through direct connection, if not by contact. It is mobile and fluid without having to stir itself. It is impersonal and at the same time clothed in personal forms. It is divisible yet whole. [...] As well as being a force it is also a milieu, a world separate from—but still in touch with—the other. [...] We might add that everything happens as if it were part of a fourth spatial dimension. An idea like mana expresses, in a way, this occult existence. (Mauss 2001, 145)

So the emphasis, here, is on mana's representation—beyond all of its different meanings—of another locus, another world in the world sustained in and by magical thinking. Yet, aside from the idea that this thinking is a collective thinking—Mauss qualifies of unconscious—which stems from its societal context, "mana [unlike its related magical practices] still seams [...] to be cut off from social life; there is something too intellectual about it," something whose status implies a sort of "judgement" (Mauss 2001, 150). As to the kind of this judgment found at the core of magical practices, and by way of questioning whether its methodology conforms to analytic and synthetic judgments, Mauss touches upon two radical factors: first, that the magician's "judgments always involve a heterogeneous term, which is irreducible to any logical analysis [...], this term is force or power, [...] or mana," those judgments are hardly analytical; and second, that "magical judgments existed prior to magical experience [...], experiences occur only in order to confirm them and almost never succeed in refuting them," thus they are not a posteriori synthetic judgments. What Mauss deduces out of those two lines is that the exception that magical thinking boils down to, and that is sustained by the function of mana, is an a priori synthetic judgment (Mauss 2001, 151–52). "The terms are connected before any kind of testing. However, it must be made clear that we have no wish to imply that magic does not demand analysis or testing. We are only saying that it is poorly analytical, poorly experimental and almost entirely a priori" (Mauss 2001, 153).

Yet, insofar as these a priori judgments are collective judgments, Mauss continues, their origin must pertain to collectivity, and he postulates that "it is only those collective needs experienced by a whole community, which can persuade all the individuals of this group to operate the same synthesis [a priori judgment] at the same time" (Mauss 2001, 154). Now, besides the fact that Mauss's attribution of this a priori judgment to such a term as "need" leaves us prey to a linear passage from nature to culture, one may extract from this last axiom that in the a priori judgment—as function ensured by mana—there is the assumption of possibility, and one that is perhaps not as scant as that of the satisfaction of the most common of needs, rather that which aims at no less than possibility as such—to use Kierkegaard's terms. For, in fact, one cannot but question, by the time a need gets common whether it would still be a need, and whether there is anything that may be called a collectivity before that point. In other words, one may question whether it is common need that implicates a priori judgment, or whether it is by a priori judgment that need becomes common—that is to say enters language to become desire.

This a priori synthetic judgment is revised by Lévi-Strauss in *Introduction to the Work of Marcel Mauss* as being split from reality (need) and as pertaining purely to the order of thinking, wherein it seems, for him, reducible to a propensity toward the "restoring of a unity; not a lost unity (for nothing is ever lost), but an unconscious one" (Lévi-Strauss 1987, 59). This unconscious unity stems, he claims, from the very identification whereby the mind associates, for instance, smoke with cloud, allowing the magician's reasoning to posit "producing smoke to elicit cloud and rain" (Lévi-Strauss 1987, 59). In other words, if a priori synthetic judgment has any foundation, Lévi-Strauss tells us, it is not to be found in the common needs that magical procedures satisfy but rather in the processes whereby the mind affords its encounter with "reality," that is to say in the mind's own reality.

From that point, Lévi-Strauss advances three axioms in preparation for his formalization of mana. First, he postulates that "language can only have arisen all at once [...] things cannot have begun to signify gradually. [...] A shift occurred from a stage when nothing had meaning to another stage when everything had meaning" (Lévi-Strauss 1987, 59). Second, he deduces that, if the outbreak of signification occurred all at once indeed, "it follows that the categories of the signifier and the signified came to be constituted simultaneously and inter-dependently, as complementary units" (Lévi-Strauss 1987, 60). And third, he advances that knowledge may be viewed as "the process which enables us to choose, from the entirety of the signifier and from the entirety of the signified, those parts which present the most satisfying relations of mutual agreement" (Lévi-Strauss 1987, 60).

Although I disagree with Lévi-Strauss, here, on his advancement of the signified as being an equivalent totality to that of the signifier (rather than a gap in it), and on that those "most satisfying relations" between signifier and signified reduce the signifier to a designative function, he produces out of these three axioms two ingenious conclusions. The first is that "the universe started signifying long before people began to know what it signified," therefore, man's first encounter with signification was an encounter with its totality (Lévi-Strauss 1987, 61). And the second is that the progress of knowledge is always a *remainder* away from this signifier-totality that "man has from the start had at his disposition. [...] There is always a non-equivalence or 'inequation' between the two, a non-fit and overspill which divine understanding alone can soak up" (Lévi-Strauss 1987, 62). So what Lévi-Strauss advances as being the locus of mana is, on the one hand, an original encounter with signification—as signifier-totality—and, on the other hand, a remainder, a gap in signification that separates knowledge from this totality.

Those two ends of man's venture in a signification whose totality he has already witnessed "generates a signifier-surfeit relative to the signifieds to which it can be fitted," Lévi-Strauss tells us, a *surplus of signification* that is mana (Lévi-Strauss 1987, 62). So it is by "the disability of all finite thought," the remainder of knowledge, that Lévi-Strauss propels his formalization of mana as a "floating signifier," which he sets up as an "expression of a semantic function, whose role is to enable symbolic thinking to operate despite the contradiction inherent in it" (Lévi-Strauss 1987, 62–63). So, if one is to summarize how Lévi-Strauss addresses this disability of thought, the matter may be brought down to an unfound signifier for a given signified, hence, the requirement of a floating signifier.

This leads Lévi-Strauss to ask how it is that mana is able to float across such diverse gaps in signification, how it manages to signify all those antinomic things. He finds himself bound to respond to this question with another formalization—namely, the *zero symbol*.

> Mana is all those [antinomic] things together; but is that not precisely because it is none of those things, but a simple form, [...] a symbol in its pure state, therefore liable to take on any symbolic content whatever? In the system of symbols which makes up any cosmology, it would just be a zero symbolic value, that is, a sign marking the necessity of a supplementary symbolic content over and above that which the signified already contains, which can be any value at all, provided it is still part of the available reserve, and is not already [...] a term in a set. (Lévi-Strauss 1987, 64)

Inasmuch as one finds the sacred, here, as simple a fact as a wait for science (whose authority along this tribute is never questioned), and insofar as authority is shown to be no more than a formal contingency that is devoid of any foundational function to language or knowledge, it is at the very point where Lévi-Strauss claims to be "rigorously faithful to Mauss's thinking" that he abandons it in the "zero symbol" (Lévi-Strauss 1987, 64). But aside from all that, one must retain from Lévi-Strauss's endeavor—and against its ambitions perhaps—that the naming of authority or possibility occurs by a signifier that "is not already a term in a set," that is to say a signifier in position of exception. Regarding the exception presented in this signifier (with reference to the master signifier that Lévi-Strauss injects in mana by this formalization), it is exception on the basis of not referring to another signifier in its set, which renders it the signifier to which all other signifiers refer. In other words, because opposition is the foundation of signification, the opposite of this signifier—mana—is opposition as such, and thus mana stands as a signifier of pure difference.

But let us return to zero symbolic value for a moment. What could a zero symbolic value possibly mean? Is it not a signifier of lack, which, although being a temporary one (for Lévi-Strauss promises its substitution by the advancement of knowledge), supposes that lack may be turned into a signifier? For to claim that in mana is no more than a zero symbolic value is to claim that knowledge, after all, manages to depart from itself, that it acquires its status away from its authorization by truth, that it has within its means a sufficient symbol to replace that which was assigned to its ontological lack, and that the symbolic, thereby, must end up hosting the real—which is reduced, then, to the fantasy of cognizance called "reality." The question of whether mana is as ideal an entity as a zero symbolic value poses, and therefore, the question of whether the relation of the signifier to the signified (and that of the symbolic to the real) is a relation—as Lévi-Strauss tells us—or a cut—as Lacan substantiates in response (Lacan 2006, 678). It also poses the question of whether language is possible as such or if it rather is only possible as discourse and thereby desire. So in zero symbolic value is laid the completeness of the symbolic, and with it the linearity of the passage between nature and culture; in sum, there is in it all that dismisses the very gap between nature and culture where our subject affords its possibility.

Zero symbolic value stands, thus, in radical antinomy with all three of the pillars of any subjective given, the *a*, the subject, and the drive; and this is why Lacan's historical battle in defense of the subject (in *Subversion of the Subject*) ends up in: "Claude Lévi-Strauss, commenting on Mauss's work, no doubt wished to see in mana the effect of a zero symbol. But it seems that what we are dealing with in our case is rather the signifier of the lack of this zero symbol" (Lacan 2006, 695). This negation whereby the *a*'s place is restituted is not only the theoretical gateway to what will further be called "the traversal of fantasy" (for this traversal is the exact opposite of any prospect of a complete symbolization as withheld in the idea of mourning). It is also as such a theoretical traversal of fantasy—namely, the fantasy whereby Lévi-Strauss posits the signifier's lack to be reducible to a signifier, the reign of the symbolic to be absolute, and, without him knowing perhaps, the lost jouissance to be negatable—by the very prospect of the complete symbolization. Another notable structuralist who does not oppose this negation any less—and one who has furnished the completeness of the symbolic with developmental stages—is Piaget. For by locating the permanence of the object in its symbolization, Piaget omits that presence—in the field of vision—is the very condition of impermanence, and omits, thereby, that permanence is reducible to absence, provided that absence is the sole ground of possibility; and this applies, in fact, as much to the visual as to the symbolic. Moreover, if there ever was such a necessity for Lacan's subversion of the Cartesian subject into a gap of the symbolic, it is precisely in that its symbolization equates its impermanence—that is to say alienation.

To return to Lacan's argument now, although he does not grant us the equivocation between mana, in its original version advanced by Durkheim and Mauss, and S(Ⱥ) or S1—due, on the one hand, to the "total social fact" Mauss binds it to, and, on the other, to Lévi-Strauss's damaging formalization in the zero symbol—he gives us every reason to believe that S(Ⱥ) is a return to Durkheim and Mauss beyond the limit imposed by Lévi-Strauss's tribute (Lacan 2006, 695).[2] The first of signifiers, Lacan tells us, is not a zero symbol, but a name of *a*—that is, in turn, the lack of a zero symbol. In other words, the first of signifiers is neither sign nor simple signifier (as in floating signifier or zero symbol); it is a name, an intermediary entity between sign and signifier where we find "the attribution that promulgates 'the dog goes meow, the cat goes woof-woof,' by which, in one fell swoop, the child, by disconnecting the thing from its cry, raises the sign to the function of the signifier and reality to the sophistics of signification" (Lacan 2006, 682). In this first naming is a cut between the sign and what it signposts—the cry and its thing—whereby the thing (i.e., jouissance) is forever negativized, for it is as absence that it is called upon by a name.

So the basic distinction introduced here—in opposition to the zero symbol—is that the name, unlike the signifier, does not correlate to something signified but to a gap or an absence in signification representing the lost jouissance; this suffices, on the one hand, for "its statement to equate its signification," and, on the other hand, for its position in signification to be that of exception (Lacan 2006, 694). So if one wants to summarize Lacan's argument against the pure symbol, one may say—using Lévi-Strauss's own terms—that it is for being rather a *symbol of the pure* than a *pure symbol* that S1 beholds its position of exception among other symbolic entities. And thus, inasmuch as this symbol of the pure (in a name) revives the sacred, the authority (i.e., possibility) that Lévi-Strauss buried in his zero symbol, one can hardly conceive of $S(\not{A})$ or S1's introduction in this argument away from a return to mana, as it was in Durkheim and Mauss's treatment, a name for pure possibility.

Yet, one doesn't only find this revival of sacredness in Lacan's introduction of S1 as name but also in the whole venture that leads him to it in *The Subversion of the Subject*; provided that this revival of Mauss's *power-milieu* forges the only root to rearticulate subject and Other on the grounds of Kierkegaard's *possibility of possibility*. For what this paper demands—if one could summarize it in a few words—is that we ask: "What else than the possibility of the subject—that is the lost jouissance—is the Other made of?" The Other, beyond its classical conception (a structure that precedes the subject) is articulated in this paper from the outset of its constitution—for the subject—as authority, the authority whereupon it gets to suppose itself as structure. "The first spoken words," Lacan tells us "decree, legislate, aphorize, and are an oracle; they give the real other its obscure authority" where there is "wholly potential power" and a "birth of possibility"—one can see here Mauss's *power-milieu* and Kierkegaard's *possibility of possibility* placed in direct equivocation (Lacan 2006, 684). One may therefore say that it is as subject (i.e., possibility of the subject) that the Other becomes Other for the subject, and further, that it is as Other (i.e., missing jouissance in the Other) that the subject becomes subject for the Other. What we have in those two operations is, on the one hand, the alienation to the "unitary trait" rendering the Other an ego-ideal, wherefrom the Other is turned into the omnipotence of the witness; and, on the other hand, the gap in this omnipotence that the subject affords, by signifying—that is to say lying—wherein they posit themself as truth (Lacan 2006, 684). In short, the relation between subject and Other becomes a relation between two gaps; one finds the Other along those lines, therefore, not less subverted than the subject, and this is precisely the point that allows us to move forward, it is the subversion, not of the subject, but of the Other.

This is the point at which the fundamental question becomes available to us: "What is the Other? What is it reducible to? Does it exist? Is it one?" For if things were left at the level of the Other as structure (as in the

Other of structural linguistics), the question would have, no doubt, been answered before being posed; but as gap, as sacredness or authority, thus, as possibility of the subject—that is, jouissance—not only does the question become possible, but it also becomes unavoidable. "Is it itself the source of its Otherness? Is it one in itself and for itself? Or is there something exceeding itself that entails the Oneness that makes its Otherness?" And thus, the question slides down the line to: "What else could have barred the subject from jouissance than the very possibility of this jouissance?"—which is Kierkegaard's pivotal axiom. And then the question becomes: "How is it that the instance that bars jouissance is, after all, the one that preserves it?" With this subversion of the Other, here, we get to the heart of the symbolic's incompleteness, for what gives it its consistency is nothing else than the real, what the Other is reducible to is not the signifier, but, in the world of the signifier, the possibility of jouissance. Here, as well, is where Lacan uncovers the radicality of the analytic act, for, provided that the Other is reducible to jouissance as possibility, it is rather extimacy than otherness; therefore, analysis is no longer the task of negativizing the lost jouissance—as Miller tells us—for that would be no more than rendering it Other, but the task of deconstructing the fantasy whereby it is positivized in (and with) the Other (Miller 2010, 83).

What derives from this conceptual advancement is that if the Name-of-the-Father has proven to render the Other at all bearable for neurosis it is not because it bars the subject from its jouissance by prohibition—for that occurs by the simple fact of speech—but because it rather bars the Other from this lost jouissance. This practically means that, with the Name-of-the-Father, the Other is rendered as much a subject of the law as the law itself. This is where Lacan advances the Other's "whimsy [alluding to the mother] that introduces the phantom of Omnipotence [...] and with this phantom, the necessity that the Other [as Law] be bridled by the Law" (Lacan 2006, 689). And departing from this necessity, he reminds us that what he had formalized of the paternal function as the Name-of-the-Father is not the rival semblable in the Oedipus myth—whose defense has praised prohibition for long—but the Freudian "dead father" whose murder instated the law (Lacan 2006, 688). For Oedipus's tragedy departs from Apollo's decree that, having kidnapped the son of Pelops, Laius shall not have a son himself, otherwise, his son would kill him and commit incest upon his mother Jocasta. In other words, what Apollo decrees is that the father must lack—the kidnapped son, if not his own, or else, he must lack as such—to establish, as name of his lacking jouissance, that is to say as desire, the order of culture by that of symbolic descendance. It is as lack, therefore, that a father ensures his function, that is, rather that of mediating jouissance by desire—which articulates it to the law—than that of legislating its annihilation, which entails finding it in effect of the legislative act. In that, inasmuch as the father is he who hosts the Other's bridling by the law within himself—wherefrom desire and law are united—the Name-of-the-Father is the name of the lacking jouissance in the Other, thus, the quilting of the signifier to its lack inscribed in S(Ⱥ)—signifier of a lack in the Other (Lacan 2006, 693–98).

In this respect, the subject's stumbling on S(Ⱥ) calls forth their lacked jouissance into the realm of signification by questioning the Other's desire "*chè voi*?"—which entails their own, for it is as Other that the subject desires (Lacan 2006, 693). In other words, in "*chè voi*?" the symbolic is accounted to answer on the mystery—as Benjamin has distinguished it from the riddle—that constitutes it as possibility, and that pertains to the real. In this call upon knowledge to say the truth about truth—"the value of the treasure trove of the signifier"—what gets put into question is the Other's very being, that is nothing else than the subject's jouissance—"what is unthinkable about him," which gets called upon in "what am I?" (Lacan 2006, 693–94). Lacan writes: "Is this Jouissance, the lack of which makes the Other inconsistent, mine [the subject's], then? Experience proves that it is usually forbidden me, not only [...] due to bad societal arrangements, but [...] because the Other is to blame—if he was to exist [*existait*], that is. But since he doesn't exist, all that's left for me is to place the blame on I, that is, to believe in what experience leads us all to, Freud at the head of the list: original sin" (Lacan 2006, 694).

What Lacan advances in those lines may be put into a logical sequence of three axioms. (1) The prohibition of jouissance stems from no "societal arrangement" that precedes it—which comes in response to the praising of prohibition—but is an effect of language, whereby "jouissance would no longer be anything but understood" (Lacan 2006, 696). In other words, "jouissance is prohibited [*interdite*] to whoever speaks, as such [...] it can only be said [*dite*] between the lines" (Lacan 2006, 696). (2)

In consequence of language's systematic reduction of jouissance to desire, it is as Other that jouissance presents itself for the subject, which entails the attribution of its consistency to the Other, and with it the blame for its loss. (3) Yet, provided that the Other doesn't exist—for, inasmuch as S1 names its lack of jouissance, the Other remains desire—the blame gets reverted on the subject in the form of the original sin, whose function is to turn the lack of jouissance (in S1) into the sacrifice that ensures its promise (or restitution), the sacrifice whereby jouissance's absence becomes the prerequisite for its permanence (Lacan 2006, 696). This *sacrifice* that occurs in the *castration complex* consists in directing the libido—preserved from its immersion in the body image—on the part that is missing in this desired image (- φ), to form the phallus Φ, as the sign that makes up for the lack of jouissance in signification (in S1) by the signaling of an ever-missing signifier, the signifier yet to come (Lacan 2006, 696–97). So, first, there is the loss of jouissance as such in its naming by S1, whereupon the law of language gets turned into the Other as desire, that is to say lack; and second, there is the restitution of jouissance as missing signifier—whose hope of finding unrolls the chain of signifiers—by its inscription through the castration complex as Φ. In other words, first, there is castration, as the Other's castration in S1 that makes him desire, and second, there is the complex that compensates this castration by Φ—that is, the jouissance the Other desires.

The crucial deduction that Lacan derives from those three axioms, and all that in sequence with the subversion of the Other into desire, the deduction that takes the neurotic a whole analysis to swallow, is that if the phallus Φ restitutes any lost jouissance, it is the Other's, for it is the Other's lost jouissance that desires in S1. In other words, insofar as lack is the Other's (in S1), Φ is its jouissance. Therefore, the neurotic imagines "that the Other demands his castration," which entails their refusal to sacrifice Φ to the Other's jouissance—this is the bedrock Freud made us pause upon in "Analysis Terminable and Interminable," and it is by this very refusal that the Other's jouissance gets preserved; for the simple fact is that fantasy, and Φ with it, is the Other's desire. Castration is, thus, "the transcendental function of ensuring the jouissance of the Other that passes this chain on to me in the Law" (Lacan 2006, 698–700). In other words, castration is the bypassing of the Other's incompleteness that satisfies the condition that it is as Other—that is to say possibility—that jouissance can be preserved.

It is at this point, in fact, that the whole problem of fantasy is revealed, not only as that which bypasses the incompleteness of the symbolic but rather as that which bypasses it to counter the incompleteness of the real—that is, jouissance not being in itself either (just like the Other), which requires its extrapolation from itself as pure possibility of itself for itself. This is where one may pick up some of the remarks that Lacan drops for us, like indices along the road, to enable our walk backward from the incompleteness of the symbolic to the incompleteness of the real. That "jouissance has to be refused in order to be attained on the inverse scale of the Law of desire" is no property that jouissance receives from the Other but is rather one that it gives (Lacan 2006, 700). For, Lacan tells us, "it is not the Law itself that bars the subject's access to jouissance—it simply makes a barred subject out of an almost natural barrier"—that is, pleasure (Lacan 2006, 696). In other words, the very problem of the real, inasmuch as its atom is the surplus there is beyond the horizon of pleasure, is that pleasure itself is its barrier, and thus that its failure is in its very success (Lacan 2006, 696). And it is this natural barrier—the barrier that is the impossibility of the real itself—that lends itself to the law of language to ensure, by the prohibition of jouissance as such, its transcription into the possibility (a signifier yet to come) whereby the brevity of autoeroticism is countered (Lacan 2006, 697). This brevity or immediacy—as the incompleteness of jouissance—is what Lacan formalizes in Seminar X in jouissance as being a falling out of the object (Lacan 2014, 175) from desire at the anxiety-point, and rearticulates in Seminar XVII as Marx's surplus value (Lacan 2007, 177) which solders its possibility to exchange—"once one has got it, it is very urgent that one squander it" for the surplus to sustain itself as possibility (Lacan 2007, 20). One cannot but underline here that if Lacan chose to ground the immediacy of jouissance in that of surplus value, things do not necessarily unfold differently for value as such. For even value is surplus value in Marx, provided that value precedes and originates the expropriation of means of production whereby the capitalist economy is launched. So, inasmuch as value itself lies in its possibility—that is the surplus, one cannot but question (in line with Mauss's articulation of value with mana) whether it really is value that explains jouissance or if it rather is jouissance that explains value.

But aside from that, jouissance being for itself rather than in itself requires us to note that the fundamental problem of analysis is neither the Other's attributed consistency—*agalma*—whose abandoning was formalized in the unbeing of the supposed subject of knowledge, nor the opacity of the castration complex that sustains—by sacrifice—this attribution, and whose seeing-through was called a traversal of fantasy; for those are only an effect and result of a more primary condition in position of cause. This condition is the real as bar to itself, it is jouissance itself as incomplete or impossible, whose correlate is the third term in the tripartite of the pass—that is subjective destitution, which was named beforehand "absolute disarray" (J. Lacan 1959–1960/2014, 304). It is from this specific standpoint—the incompleteness of jouissance as cause—that one is required to approach, and with great care, the last lines of *The Subversion of the Subject* where Lacan advances that "coming to terms with the Other" lies in "experiencing not the Other's demand, but its will [...] to castrate [...], which leads to the supreme narcissism of the Lost Cause (the latter being the path of Greek tragedy, which Claudel rediscovers in a Christianity of despair)" (Lacan 2006, 700). For this Lost Cause is what Claudel defines for us as the "third sin."

> Let us die then, for it is easier to be flat on one's face than standing,
> Less easy to live than to die, and on the cross than under it.
> Save us from the Third sin, which is despair! (Claudel 2016, 182)

By assigning to despair the status of a third sin, Claudel doesn't only equate despair to disbelief; rather more, he situates in despair the consummation of the principle of sacrifice there is in the original sin, the sacrifice whereby the loss of jouissance becomes the foundation of its promise. For Jesus lies "all alone like Adam [...] and savors the Wine, the invincible ignorance of man in the withdrawal of God!" (Claudel 2016, 184). In other words, what Christ endures in despair is jouissance as such, the invincible ignorance that is his immediacy. In that, as "He savors slowly the cup and the death that poisons Him," jouissance gets revealed to him as the incompleteness there is in that it is only enjoyment where one no longer is to enjoy; which poses the question of whose enjoyment it is, as much when jouissance gets endured as such than when it gets quilted to the signifier by the medium of sacrifice (Claudel 2016, 184). In other words, regardless of whether one sacrifices it to the Lord's promise (as in the original sin) or dissolves in it its sacrifice (as in the third sin), it remains as much in its final than in its initial term (whether mediated or immediate) the Other's jouissance.

> Have You then not enough of that sour wine mixed with water,
> That You suddenly straighten up and cry: Sitio?
> You are thirsty, Lord? Is it to me You are speaking?
> Is it I that you need still and my sins?
> Is it I who am missing before all is consummated? (Claudel 2016, 184)

What gets voiced out in Jesus's last words, right before becoming signifier, is not "*ché voi*?"; for, at the bottom of one's destitution one doesn't ask the Lord "What do you want from me?" one rather answers it: "Don't you see, Lord, that the jouissance you want is my destitution?" Or, to use the brutal scansion whereby Freud ends his *Interpretation of Dreams*, "Father can't you see, I'm burning."

What one ends up with, by following desire till its end, is that the jouissance one was after is the Other's—a necessity forged by its incompleteness—and that, thus, it is one's own destitution—which Claudel calls a "consummation." This is a fact that mustn't sound like a novelty for whoever departs from Freud's primitive scene (the fundamental fantasy) whereby a child imagines jouissance's possibility as the Other's, which serves them well in posing their destitution, their falling like an excrement from the ultimate jouissance of their beloved with their rival, as the initial and final term of infernal enjoyment—that is, humiliation. It is that, that Lacan calls upon where he speaks of submitting oneself to "the Other's will to castrate" by becoming "the mummy of some Buddhist initiation" (Lacan 2006, 700). On that, if we were to pay our real dues to Melanie Klein—away from praising any ideology of renunciation—we'd have to recognize in her paranoid-schizoid state the earlier works of the primitive scene, whereby jouissance is deposited as possibility in all the might of the bad frustrating breast and is split from the meagerness of that good breast that provides no more than pleasure. In other words, what Klein has shown us with utmost accuracy is that there is no primitive scene before which jouissance was possible by other means than pain, and that its possibility has always occurred, and since the very start, by repetition, that the primitive scene is already a repetition.

To return to Claudel now, besides the fact that one finds in his lines sufficient insight on the clinical ambition there is in subjective destitution, what he offers us in the most exact of manners is the measure whereby belief, and with it certainty, is turned into conviction—conviction being the scar of analysis that Freud introduced in all the fog of "Analysis Terminable and Interminable" (Freud 1964, 252). It is the conviction that jouissance is in any case incomplete and in both cases the Other's, as well as that sacrifice—whether within or without belief—is its necessity, provided that jouissance's possibility can occur by no other medium than desire. This is an idea that Lacan puts in ironically simple words toward the end of *The Ethics of Psychoanalysis*: "One should call things by their name [...]: psychoanalysis teaches that in the end it is easier to accept interdiction than to run the risk of castration" (Lacan 1992, 307).

In other words, analysis teaches that the inconsistency of the interdicted—whose only possible completeness is in its positivization, as in the complex—renders interdiction more tolerable than the pain of jouissance. Furthermore, having shown in the sustainment of the completeness of jouissance (as *happiness*) the most austere of the superego's injunctions (*the Sovereign* Good), Lacan assigns to the analyst (in *The Ethics of Psychoanalysis*) no other criterion of formation than their conviction that it does not exist—which is, in effect, the traversal of fantasy he introduces later on (Lacan 1992, 299). Lacan also rearticulates this point in a formalization at the very end of *Seminar on Anxiety*; a formalization which, by intending to address the conviction that allows a subject to insure a paternal function, does not only reveal that which insures the analytic function, but also that which analysis produces in whoever withstands it.

> Contrary to what religious myth states, the father is not a causa sui, but a subject who has gone far enough into the realization of his desire to be able

> to integrate it back into its cause, whatever that may be, back into what is irreducible in the function of the *a*. This is what allows us to link in with the very principle of our research, without eluding it in any way, the fact that there is no human subject who does not have to posit himself as an object, a finite object, to which his finite desires are appended, desires which only look like they are infinite inasmuch as, in each getting farther away from their center, they carry the subject farther away from any authentic realization. (Lacan 2014, 337)

What "going far enough into the realization of desire" produces—this far enough realization being destitution—is desire's reintegration into its cause; a reintegration that entails the conviction that desire is made to *sustain* rather than *attain*, provided that its object—that is, the subject as jouissance—is only possible (if not bearable) in the form of its lack. So if it is conviction that analysis produces—the conviction wherein Freud introduced all three of the pillars of absolute knowing, as we've seen in the previous chapter—it is the conviction that jouissance is castration itself. What Lacan offers by situating destitution as the outcome of analysis is no beyond castration, rather a beyond the complex, that is, in turn, a negation of the beyond castration as function. It is, in fact, a *rescuing of castration* that analysis can afford.

Should this not make us wonder, again, why such a man as Oedipus decides, at the moment he recognizes the blindness there is in the midst of all his sight, to realize it by plucking out his eyes? For what else does his act render visible than a blindness that is already there, and, most importantly, to whom does it make this blindness visible—for he has seen it already? One may therefore wonder if it is only about giving up the thing that captivated him—jouissance—to enter the zone of pursuing desire, as Lacan tells us, or if it is rather about giving his blindness the irreversible stature of evidence—the sole constituent of conviction (Lacan 1992, 304). For why would one rid oneself of a gaze that is already blind if one was to remain as blind as one already was? And what else than desire did Oedipus end up with, in his pursuit of the thing, even before turning his blindness of sight into the sight of blindness? As captivated as one may be by that thing, it only works as a cause of one's desire, for one doesn't get to any greater enjoyment than pain. So the act at stake is not as simple as that which separates dwelling in jouissance from becoming a subject of desire—a reading that supposes that desire is such a sufficient solution to the matter anyway; it is rather the act that reveals desire, whether the one that precedes or succeeds it, as eternally being the Other's desire. For where Oedipus pleads "I am not guilty," he attests, "it was not I who desired"; it is to that that he was blind, and, for that, willing to blind himself even more for the chorus to see. Therefore, as if to assume his castration, Oedipus chooses to turn his blindness into the evidence that desire was the Other's all along. What he engraves in his body by plucking out his eyes is the sign of lack in the Other—and that, neither signifier nor deception, it is a symptom; the scar whereupon one reintegrates the whole tragedy on the conviction that it has always been already ended. In short, desire is the path of the law, it is a forced choice.[3]

And thus, if the primitive scene is not that primitive after all, if the primitive scene is already a repetition, then the fundamental fantasy is rather what is fundamental to fantasy than a fundamental fantasy; which—in line with Zupančič's disquisition we followed in the first chapter—is the very postulation of the possibility of the one in that of the final end, that is, lack's complete and consummated positivization. In that, what of fantasy gets traversed in destitution, and whose inscription is the conviction that Oedipus engraves in a symptom, is the belief that fantasy—and with it desire—may lead to any other end than their very start and repetition. That is why Oedipus chooses to sacrifice, in spite of his blindness, what is left of his sight, in virtue of the truth that desire, being the Other's, knows no other end than its repetition—there was no further destiny Oedipus could see for Athens than that.

One can hardly conceive Lacan's advancement of destitution—which states that the encounter of the incompleteness of the symbolic has no other medium than the incompleteness of the real—as being a rupture with the dialectic; it is rather a return to the dialectic. That many have followed the temptation to hear in the traversal of fantasy the means of transcendence is their own business, and one which is hardly sustainable, anyway, without societal arrangements. In truth, nothing of what Lacan advances here would have sounded misplaced for Hegel, not even where he challenges Hegelianism in uncovering the double edge of desire—"The work, Hegel tells us, to which the slave submits in giving up jouissance out of fear of death, is precisely the path by which he achieves freedom" (Lacan 2006, 686). For, indeed, a nonideological end to analysis cannot but align itself with the unfeasibility of any stable finitude to ideology. What we'd fall into, otherwise, by turning the *event* of uncommodification into the *possibility* of a supreme commodity, is the political category Lacan has called *les-non-dupes-errent*—which entails that one who considers themself to have broken free from ideology for good (becoming *non-dupe*) are the one trapped in it the most (they *err*). On that, whereas Lacan leads us to the conclusion that the dialectic closes itself on no more than a *symptom*—conviction—that opens it up anew, Hegel tells us that self-equality (or the absolute concept) does not precede the dialectic, provided that the self-equal first presents itself as already estranged, and that it becomes self-equal only as a result of the dialectic; that is to say, becoming self-equal is another estrangement that operates a deestrangement—it is therefore a symptom (Hegel 2018, 99). Therefore, against the view that finds greater ambitions than a symptom, and always, on the grounds of some totalization of the law, one must recall that the Babylonian legislation is accountable enough for that the law itself originated as a symptom, and that symptom is the only law there is—the sovereignty of lack being the sole foundation for any justice. What else than a dead end would comfort the *experience* of such a misadventure as an ending analysis—not to mention the one it leads to? One finds a slightly better outlook of repeating differently in a dead end than in no end at all, especially when one admits what is a fact—namely, that analysis was never a *choice*.

Notes

1. Identification—whether imaginary or symbolic identification—can neither resolve the Oedipus complex nor what has preceded it, provided it maintains lack as positivized by the supposition that the rapport between mother and father is satisfactory. That is to say, identification maintains the conception of the Other's desire as being a demand.
2. Although the signifier of lack in the other S(Ⱥ) and the first signifier S1 are terms Lacan introduced at different moments of his theoretical trajec-

tory, in sequence with the quilting point and the Name-of-the-Father, the main endeavor he offers in *The Subversion of the Subject and the Dialectic of Desire* assembles them as successive axioms of a single concept, inasmuch as they all address the function of authority in the establishment of discourse. It is in this manner that those concepts are referred to as being equivalent.

3. I quote an analysand, here, who writes me a message about the *strangeness* of desire after a year in *destitution*: "It's day zero at kindergarten. The weather reminds me of a very basic configuration, and smells mix. There are wooden shapes, cylinders in yellow, green triangles, and the smell of modeling clay. Such a relief, such a basic configuration. But it also appears the world has configured itself in such strange complex forms, a prison, a school, a job, strange desires."

References

Claudel, Paul. 2016. The Way of the Cross (1867–1955). Translated by John Dunaway. *Logos* 19 (2, Spring): 177–186.

Dolar, Mladen. 2005. Nothing Has Changed. *Filozofski Vestnik* 26 (2): 147–160.

Dor, Joël. 2001. *Structure and Perversions*. New York: Other Press.

Durkheim, Emile. 1915. *The Elementary Forms of the Religious Life*. Translated by Joseph Ward Swain. London: George Allen and Unwin.

Freud, Sigmund. 1964. Analysis Terminable and Interminable. In *Moses and Monotheism, An Outline of Psycho-Analysis, and Other Works*, vol. 23 of The Standard Edition of the Complete Psychological Works of Sigmund Freud. Translated by James Strachey. London: Hogarth Press.

———. 2000–2010b. From the History of an Infantile Neurosis, (1918). In *Freud: Complete Works*, translated and edited by Ivan Smith. https://www.valas.fr/IMG/pdf/Freud_Complete_Works.pdf.

———. 2000–2010c. A Seventeenth-Century Demonological Neurosis. (1923). In *Freud: Complete Works*, translated and edited by Ivan Smith. 2000, 2007, 2010. https://www.valas.fr/IMG/pdf/Freud_Complete_Works.pdf.

———. 2000–2010d. Some Psychical Consequences of The Anatomical Distinction Between The Sexes. (1925). In *Freud: Complete Works*, translated and edited by Ivan Smith. https://www.valas.fr/IMG/pdf/Freud_Complete_Works.pdf.

———. 2000–2010e. An Outline of Psycho-Analysis (1940). In *Freud: Complete Works*, translated and edited by Ivan Smith. https://www.valas.fr/IMG/pdf/Freud_Complete_Works.pdf.

———. 2000–2010f. Splitting of the Ego in the Process of Defence (1940). In *Freud: Complete Works*, translated and edited by Ivan Smith. https://www.valas.fr/IMG/pdf/Freud_Complete_Works.pdf.

Harari, Roberto. 2001. *Lacan's Seminar on "Anxiety": An Introduction"*. Cambridge: Other Press.

Hegel, Georg Wilhelm Fredrich. 2018. *The Phenomenology of Spirit.* Translated by Terry Pinkard and Michael Baur. Cambridge: Cambridge University Press.

Kierkegaard, Søren. 1957. *The Concept of Dread.* Translated by Walter Lowrie. Princeton: Princeton University Press.

Lacan, Jacques. 1962–1963/1981. *The Four Fundamental Concepts of Psychoanalysis.* The Seminar of Jacques Lacan, vol. XI. Edited by Jacques-Alain Miller and translated by Alan Sheridan. New York: W. W. Norton.

———. 1992. *The Ethics of Psychoanalysis, 1959–1960.* The Seminar of Jacques Lacan, vol. VII. Edited by Jacques-Alain Miller and translated by Dennis Porter. New York: W. W. Norton.

———. 2006. *Ecrits: The First Complete Edition in English.* Edited and translated by Bruce Fink. New York: W. W. Norton.

———. 2007. *The Other Side of Psychoanalysis.* The Seminar of Jacques Lacan, Vol. XVII. Edited by Jacques-Alain Miller, Translated by Russel Grigg. New York: W. W. Norton.

———. 1959–1960/2014. *Anxiety.* The Seminar of Jacques Lacan, vol. X. Edited by Jacques-Alain Miller and translated by A. R. Price. Cambridge: Polity Press.

Lévi-Strauss, Claude. 1987. *Introduction to the Work of Marcel Mauss (1950).* Translated by Felicity Baker. London: Routledge & Kegan Paul.

Mauss, Marcel. 1923. Essai sur le don forme et raison de l'échange dans les sociétés archaïques. *L'Année sociologique (1896/1897–1924/1925)* 1: 30–186.

———. 2001. *A General Theory of Magic.* Translated by Robert Brain. London: Routledge.

Miller, Jacques-Alain. 2010. Extimité: extrait du cours de l'année 1985–1986: séance du 27 novembre 1985. *Letterina* 55 (56): 13–27.

4

The Procedure, from Solution to Dissolution

"There is only one kind of psychoanalysis, the training analysis" (Lacan 1981, 274). Are we not fortunate that Lacan enounced this declaration—in Seminar XI—before he started scribbling the first draft of his "October Proposition 1967"? But we are not fortunate because it simply denounces once more the orthodox hegemony that established itself on the ideal of a stand-alone didactic analysis—a matter that has been given due attention elsewhere. The fortune in this announcement is that it declares once and for all that psychoanalysis is what retroactively proves to have always already been didactic. In other words, that psychoanalysis is what proves to have amended the Other by a symptom, the symptom whose most radical form is appointing oneself as the bearer and witness of the imposture that sustains the Other's existence—that is to say, authorizing oneself to exert the analytic function. Have we not had enough, therefore, from reading this proposition as Lacan demanded back then "against the background of […] 'Situation de la psychanalyse et formation du psychanalyste en 1956'" (Lacan 2009, 1). For there is far more in this procedure than an answer to the societal misadventure of the formation of the analyst. If the formation of the analyst is the only analysis there is, then this proposition of the pass is not exactly the procedure which guarantees the

M. Tal, *The End of Analysis*, The Palgrave Lacan Series,
https://doi.org/10.1007/978-3-031-29889-9_4

becoming of the analyst but rather the one that appoints to the analysand's endeavor its very finality—the analytic symptom.

This is where the term "procedure" is able to recover its true weight in fact, for there is more sense to "procedure" than whichever institutional arrangement—the pass—Lacan comes to propose. If the formation of the analyst is the only analysis there is, then where one expects a concept of an end to analysis, it is a procedure that one gets. And this is a question that must be addressed with great care, for no other part of Lacan's writings carries greater commitment than that which "proposition" assigns and "dis-solution" inscribes.[1] No other part of Lacan's theoretical trajectory has ever proposed an establishment of procedural body. And if this procedure of the pass proclaims to guarantee—in effect—the end of analysis by the formation of the analyst who directs it (the so-called analyst of the school, or AE), its core aims are reverse; that is, it guarantees the formation of this analyst of the school with the end of his own analysis.

So, to pose the question as one must: Why is it that Lacan corners us in such a harsh bargain? Why is it that he decides to provide a procedure where we demand a concept? In short, the dialectic is to blame; the problem of psychoanalysis cannot be addressed by knowledge; rather, it is that which must be addressed in knowledge as truth—that is, the jouissance the Other stands for, agalma. In other words, it is the real's incompleteness that necessitates the symbolic as its locus. Therefore, concept is no better of an answer than procedure; besides that, concept is only concept in retrospect from procedure on itself, that is to say that a concept is itself a procedure. This chapter aims to demonstrate, departing from what has preceded, how the pass (as production of the sinthome) offers the sole nonideological concept of the finality of analysis, through amending transference rather than fantasizing its liquation.

Impossible Transference and the Cartesian Prospect

The actual deadlock that the proposition departs from is not in the first pages where Lacan proposes "gradus" in contradiction to "rank" (Lacan 2009, 1). Lacan's aim here is to disrupt the real's "systematic negation" or "misrecognition" in psychoanalytic societies (Lacan 2009, 3). Nor is the deadlock in the second opposition that he posits right afterward between "psychoanalysis in extension" and "psychoanalysis in intention" (Lacan 2009, 4). Rather, the deadlock only comes into play with the third opposition that Lacan introduces, between *therapeutics* and *psychoanalysis*, the opposition by which he intends to dismantle the long-preserved division of analysis between therapeutic analysis and didactic analysis.

> This experience is essential to isolate it from therapeutics, which does not distort psychoanalysis only by relaxing its rigor. I will note in effect that there is no possible definition of the therapeutic other than the reinstating of the first condition. A definition that is precisely impossible to pose in psychoanalysis. As for the primum non nocere, let us not mention it, for it is changeable in not being able to be determined as primum at the start: what are we to choose not to harm! Just try. It is too easy in this condition to set to the credit of any treatment whatsoever the fact that it has not harmed something. This compulsory feature is of interest only because it depends on an undecidable logic. We can find the time, now over (*révolu*), when what it was a matter of not harming was the morbid entity. (Lacan 2009, 5)

So, "there is only one kind of psychoanalysis, the training analysis," provided that normality is only retroactively produced by the medium of its loss (a sufficient condition for its infinite reproduction), and that therapeutic analysis—inasmuch as therapeutic means reinstating the first condition—is then reduced to fantasy (Lacan 1981, 274). Nevertheless, it is absolutely necessary to address how it is the dialectic of the drive that gets assigned here with the task of negating normality: First, insofar as psychoanalysis (as opposed to therapeutics) finds, no first condition it can reinstate—for this first condition is only a fact of the second, that is division—what psychoanalysis is bound to address is a dialectic. And second, what constitutes an origin for this dialectic, and which therapeutics got established around the prerogative of not harming, is harm itself, "the morbid entity," that is negation. In other words, as long as subjectivity is the unfolding of the dialectic of negation (the drive), normality is not lost normality but rather one that is ever to come.

The most direct consequence of those two axioms, however, is that although an analytic venture always departs from a decision, the analysand's decision, nothing permits us to equate this decision with any kind of choice. For as long as it is a drive that subtends the speaking subject, which suffices to turn desire's ever-missed encounter with its cause into a questioning of being (what am I?), analysis is the only possible unfolding of its dialectic. Consequently, division, desire, transference, and analysis are all one and the same result; let us rid our minds therefore of this cliché once and for all: analysis is not a choice provided that all subjects are divided subjects and thereby analysands. On these grounds, we can assign to therapeutics their correct standpoint, which is a suspension of analysis in intent; for therapeutics all responds to affect by sealing the question opened by desire's impossibility (what am I?). On that, we should oppose Aron Schuster's qualification of analysis as "anti-therapy," for as long as one departs from the ontological fact that binds us to repetition, it is rather therapy that is to be considered as anti-analysis than the reverse (Schuster 2017, 91).

Now this is where one grasps why Lacan decides to aim at the end of analysis in this proposition through no other entry point than its beginning (i.e., a nonbeginning), the beginning he denotes as distinct from the person of the analyst on the grounds that transference constitutes by itself the principal of nonrelation (Lacan 2009, 5). Lacan even willingly throws the whole affair of choosing an analyst on luck, for besides the function that makes the analyst what they are at the start—and which necessarily precedes the analyst—the rest is all reducible to contingency (Lacan 2009, 5). Therefore, analysis is not a choice, as we said earlier, and the analyst even less; provided the analyst and the clinical situation they institute are only introduced as a frame for a transference and analysis that precede them and that originate from no other fact than division—the division which Dolar properly substantiates as a nonbeginning, or a failure to begin being by any consummated end of nonbeing (Dolar 2018, 18).

So why wouldn't we disturb with such an assertion the light-hearted analyst who reduce transference to the analytical instrument of the healer they take themself to be? Should we not allege in response that transference is all there is among speaking subjects, and that everyday speech—were it not to the societal mechanisms sustaining its lure of intersubjectivity—would tumble by itself into the plea we hear every day in a clinic, if not a church? Should we not recall here that Freud had no other intent in introducing a couch into his praxis than that of hiding the trouble of being pondered by hysterics as the actual addressee of their speech? That is to say that if the divan retained its use in analysis over more than a century, it is not for inducing any extraordinary effect to speech but rather for bringing it down by the most artificial setting there is to its most ordinary condition—that is, that regardless of who's actually listening it is always to God that one speaks (Lacan 2009, 7). In other words, the divan is the necessary artifact that reveals the most ordinary state of speech (i.e., transference) and which derives from the unfeasibility of intersubjectivity—given the property of the signifier—wherein language could have operated as communication.

Furthermore, where Freud reveals in transference the experiment of reproducing ordinary love, he confronts us with the question whether there is anything in ordinary love that is not already a transference (Lacan 2011, 53). This is a point Seminar VIII takes up when retracing from Alcibiades's love for Socrates to the formalization of transference as "transference-love," which precisely states that none of those two terms can ever do away with the other, provided they are complementary approaches of the same deadlock in the real which makes desire resort to the Other's desire—that is to say lack—as its sole possibility (Lacan 2011, 147–53). Therefore, nothing should prevent us from questioning whether there ever was a neurosis that—as uninvolved in analysis as it may seem to be—was not already a *transference neurosis*; what is it that an analysand comes to complain about in analysis otherwise, if not what already is well before analysis the transference neurosis—that is to say the burden of an ever-failing love?

Our question is henceforth bound to undergo a radical twist, for insofar as one departs from the idea that analysis and transference have always already been there with division and desire, the question becomes, "To what term can analysis bring a situation of which (as opposed to therapeutics) it is a result?" In other words, "What term can analysis bring (not to transference, but) into transference, without falling into the fantasy—withheld in every idea of its liquidation—of realizing disentanglement by intersubjectivity?" (Lacan 2009, 14). That is why, if one is to address the specific moment where Lacan brings his subject supposed to know into the equation, the least one could say is that he brings it in precisely to do away with the liquidation of transference—for what on earth is not transference if intersubjectivity is no possible alternative (Lacan 2009, 9)? Even more, this proposition makes sure to denote that if anything sustains any desire to know in the analyst, it still is agalma, which rather is in the analysand than in the analyst—in other words, that there is no less transference in the analyst than in anybody else (Lacan 2009, 16).

But let us pause on the problem of transference as we must, for if it is evident for us now that there is no other to transference (i.e., love), that doesn't make transference possible. On that, if Freud has managed to reveal greater authority in the totem than in the mythical father (hence the utility of his murder), it only serves in confirming that the father was already another totem for his rulership to have prevailed in the first place. This implies in turn—and Mauss would not agree more—that no primitive horde was ever primitive enough for the transferred not to have occurred itself by transference, nor to not have required afterward another transference; therefore, that transference can never be complete. In other words, that transference has always ended up being a retransference constitutes sufficient evidence of its very impossibility. In practical terms, against the widespread idea that transference is some repetition of one's first relation to one's mother and father, we must underline that Freud's use of the notion of *parental imagos* asserts enough that those parental figures are already a transference. Therefore, if mother (for instance) is only mother by transference, why would there be a transference beyond her if not for the fact that transference can never be complete? So on the one hand we have the fact that there is no other to transference, and on the other hand we have the fact that there is no other to transference precisely because transference is impossible, because it is always incomplete, it is always a retransference. This is a point Freud hints at by qualifying as "impossible" the three professions which, established as authorities on the foundation of transference, remain ordained by its own impossibility—that Schuster formalizes as "a 'critical ateleology' that suspends [...] the usual goal-oriented mindset and thereby opens a unique space in which something else can occur" (Schuster 2017, 99).

Let us acknowledge, therefore, that it is not transference that constitutes the problem of psychoanalysis (for there is nothing else than transference) but its impossibility, the impossibility of a complete and consummated transference—which, had it been possible, would have enabled transference to exceed itself and constitute the subject as a given. To put it in practical terms, one does not go to analysis because one is in transference (for who isn't?); one goes to analysis because transference doesn't work, because transference isn't transference enough to produce a subject once and for all. And this is a point Lacan explains in Seminar XI by underlining that the certainty Descartes retroacts from doubt can never be an acquired certainty; it is a certainty that never becomes a given inasmuch as the subject he manages to become certain about in that moment of the cogito is a negativity, and one that is already missed; it is on those grounds that Lacan tells us that Descartes's "mistake is to believe that this [certainty] is knowledge" (Lacan 1981, 224). "Certainty, for Descartes, is not a moment that one may regard as acquired, once it has been crossed. Each time and by each person it has to be repeated. It is an ascesis. It is a point of orientation that is particularly difficult to sustain in the incisiveness that makes its value. It is, strictly speaking, the establishment of something separate" (Lacan 1981, 224). And all that boils down to the fact that, in retrospect from any posteriority of enunciation, the subject of enunciation is only graspable as subject of the enounced, that is to say ego. As Martial Gueroult puts it, although Descartes does offer us the path to certainty, he does not lure us with the possibility of its doubling—that is, to be certain about certainty after it has occurred (Gueroult 1984, 92). Thus, where Descartes pronounces God as undeceiving, that is to say as being desire (in correlation to certainty), he does not exclude in any way the return of the lure of the Evil Genius—that is the Other's completeness that is posited in intentionality—offering us the path, thereby, to conceive the dawn of Enlightenment and that of repetition as being one and the same. That is to say, what Enlightenment is about, after the frivolity of Renaissance, was that the new (which is henceforth a negativity) only occurs through repetition; a point that is necessary to retain for us to resituate psychoanalysis in its correct order, that is, as outcome—if not as revival—of the Enlightenment project.

This unfolding of the constancy of transference out of its own impossibility is an axiom we must take very seriously. Not only is it the core of Enlightenment that Hegel crystallizes later in his dialectic, which derives from the fact that negation is always a failed negation; this axiom is also the fundamental element Lacan injects at the start of his proposition to make sure destitution is not summoned as some experience of disentanglement from the object (or from transference). And that, provided that which hasn't properly started—that is the strict definition of division—cannot afford to end, but can only symptomatize. In other words, this is the axiom wherefrom the "October Proposition" and the production of the Sinthome may be grasped—despite being ten years apart from one another—as being one and the same procedure.

Now let us turn our attention to the locus of this certainty that Descartes couldn't do without introducing with the idea of the undeceiving God. If Descartes's certainty couldn't do without God's will (for he postulates that if he reached certainty by pure reason then God wants him to), it is because the "I doubt," by the fact that Descartes enounces it, already supposes a locus of signification wherein the signifier represents him—as speaking subject—for another signifier, which results in turn in the "I am." Yet, this handing back of truth to God as omnipotence, which Descartes demonstrates departing from the theory of eternal truths, leaves us prey to a positivization of this locus, which Lacan addresses by underlining that what is at stake in this omnipotence "is a question not so much of a perfect, as of an infinite being," that is to say a locus of the real, that is a negativity (Gueroult 1984, 23; Lacan 1964/1981, 225). Those are the grounds on which one may grasp Lacan's reintroduction of the subject supposed to know in the "October Proposition," first as being not a subject but rather a locus of truth by which the subject may subtract itself from the knowledge that alienates it; and second as being supposed by nothing else than the signifier which, by supposing it, also supposes the knowledge that constitutes alienation—that is, the Freudian unconscious. As Lacan writes:

> Is it now possible to doubt that in referring what the unconscious uncovers for us to the subject of the cogito [...], I sufficiently indicate that no subject is supposable by another subject,—if this term must indeed be taken

> from Descartes's angle. That he required God or rather the truth with which he credits him, for the subject to come and lodge itself under the same cloak that clothes deceptive human shadows—that Hegel in taking it up again poses the impossibility of the coexistence of consciousnesses, in as far as it concerns the subject destined for knowledge [...], to whoever knows how to form it. (Lacan 2009, 6)

Where all the stress is being laid here is the fact that what the cogito involves of God in the production of certainty is not God as subject but quite the reverse; it is as truth that God is called forth for the subject to be subtracted from knowledge in "I am." Furthermore, the fact that the signifier by itself supposes this locus of truth, whereby it represents the subject for another signifier (Lacan 2009, 7), does not only oppose any possible wish to settle the matter with intersubjectivity; it also constitutes the foundational element for Hegelian dialectics—which formalize "the impossibility of the coexistence of consciousnesses." For why would there be a dialectic if consciousness was not already the Other's? So first, the subject supposed to know is not a subject, but a locus of the subject; second, it is supposed by nothing else than the signifier; and now third, what is it exactly supposed to know?

Answering this question requires us to depart again from Descartes's desire, which, despite considering his certainty as being a knowledge of pure reason, reveals that the real venture in his *Meditations* was to uncover, well beyond knowledge, truth in his actions—that is, to uncover what he was as desire (Lacan 1981, 222). The desire he touches upon by pointing out in doubt his freedom of will, which he realigns with the infinite will of God—desire, in other words, being the Other's desire (Gueroult 1984, 42–108). Thus, if one could summarize Descartes's response to skepticism (the subjective position that we can know nothing), it would not be the simplistic affirmation that there is something that can be known apart from the deficiency of our senses, for knowledge alienates us already to the point of rendering us immune to perception; rather, on the contrary, Descartes's response to skepticism might be summarized by saying that there is already too much knowledge (i.e., alienation) in us for us to reach certainty (i.e., separation) by any other mean than doubt—and that is what paved our way to the Cartesian methodological doubt we owe the

Enlightenment on the one hand and modernity on the other (Lacan 1981, 222–23; Gueroult 1952/1984, 24–92).

The matter we must address here is whether the cogito stands as one or minus one (a positive addition or a subtraction) in relation to knowledge; whether Descartes's certainty stands as a dent in knowledge as he claimed in that first instant of realization or as a foundation upon which knowledge was to be reconquered by pure reason as he reiterated later on—by assigning to the truth he credited God with the totalizing means of objective validity. Distinguishing those two trajectories of methodological doubt (first the conceptual procedure provided by the project of Enlightenment and second the unfolding of modern science out of this project and in contrast with it) is unavoidable if one is to escape such a misfortunate beginning as that which Foucault announces in *the death of man*; for (when read as minus one) the cogito translates into the exact opposite of this declaration, that *man is strictly undead* (in the Hegelian sense) provided their being subject relies on doubting their own death in knowledge from its very outset.

What follows from this distinction is the question whether the subject of the cogito was a subject of science whose necessary counterpart is the complete Other, which warrants objective validity by reducing truth to a formal cause, or a subject of the unconscious whose Other is the gap of desire—as locus of truth—generative of discourse (Chiesa 2016, 41). On that, it suffices that one departs from Lorenzo Chiesa's classification of the subject of science as repression and that of the unconscious as return of the repressed for one to grasp the subject brought forward by the cogito as being already a return of the repressed, whose negativity persists no more than the instant of it being missed, and which causes in turn yet another repression—namely, that of modern science (Chiesa 2016, 43). This is a point Chiesa touches upon further departing from the theory of the four discourses by formalizing the intertwining there is between "the One's production" and the "production of the One" in logic and discourse (Chiesa 2016, 151). Thus, we won't settle for the idea that the subject of the unconscious is only allowed against the background of the subject of science—a view we can only have from the outset of the cogito's aftermath—for that would undermine the true weight of the cogito at the moment where it occurred in Descartes's reasoning. What the cogito uncovered in its first instance was that the subject of consciousness conceived by skepticism—as de facto divided from knowledge—was already alienated enough to knowledge for that knowledge (the meditator knows not that they know) to be taken for perception. And it is in that that the subject of the cogito may be apprehended as being the subject of the unconscious before getting to be that of science, provided Descartes announces in it that the modern man—Freud declared later on as *analysand*—is rather burdened by knowledge than by ignorance; and that, by this very fact, their deestrangement was to be henceforth brought by methodological doubt, that is the sole path of their desire (Lacan 1981, 224).

Let us affirm thereon that if this *subject supposed to know*—the ego-ideal—holds any function in relation to knowledge, it would not be that of representing anything to be known but rather the initial *not-known* that made the exception (in S1) wherefrom alienation (i.e., discourse) originated at the start. In other words, the subject supposed to know is the exact reverse of any promise of knowledge; it is rather a promise of getting done with knowledge by the medium of truth—that is to say, a promise of a complete and consummated separation from knowledge, or, better still, a guarantee of a final disentanglement of being from structure.

It is only from this point, now, that we may access Lacan's additional reading of the cogito in *La Logique du Fantasme*, not as *inversion* of the plane of alienation introduced in Seminar XI, as François Balmès argues, but as consequence (Balmès 2011, 21). For if alienation is indeed alienation to knowledge, as Seminar XI introduced, it can only operate on the foundation of the subject supposed to know, that is, in turn, the supposed potentiality of separation from knowledge that renders knowledge supposable in the first place. In other words, alienation in knowledge boils down to alienation in being, provided it is subtended by the subject supposed to know—that is to say that structure is henceforth real (Chiesa 2016, 44). This is a point Balmès extracts from *La Logique du Fantasme* where the subject supposed to know is formalized as a primordial *conjunction of thinking and being* that instigates their very *disjunction* as foundation for subjectivity (Balmès 2011, 34). Yet what unfolds from this axiom is that the being and the thinking that Descartes aspired to tie together in his cogito are disjoined orders by the fact they are founded on mutual negation. Hence, being can only subjectivize as "I do not think" and thinking as "I am not," which doubles the alienation that subjectivity presupposes by that "either I do not think or I am not"—that is to say that neither being nor thinking can exceed the threshold of potentiality provided none of them is in itself (Lacan 2010b, 51–65).

Lacan rearticulates on the basis of this the idea of defense as imaginary (in *I do not think*) and resistance as symbolic (in *I am not*) to address the problem of subjectivity as the subject's double aphanisis—either by resistance or by defense—insofar as being asserts itself as little in the unconscious as in fantasy (Lacan 2010b, 52). For, provided the subject of the unconscious "limits the establishment of being as such to that of the 'I am' implied by the pure functioning of the subject of the 'I think'"—Lacan qualifies it rather as *am-thinking* than *I am*—it is rejected through fantasy's reiteration of the subject as ego, that is to say the object *a* the Other lacks (Lacan 2010b, 59). Thus, instead of exceeding the missed being of the unconscious by any brighter state of being, fantasy only brings it down to nonbeing of the object *a*. And it is there, from the imaginary deadlock of consciousness—that is the rejection of thought whereby the subject is reduced to the object *a* (i.e., nonbeing)—that thinking returns as unconscious to reinstate the Other's lack by transference, as the sign of a missed being—countering, thereby, nonbeing by missed being again (Lacan 2010b, 166).

The matter is to be apprehended here rather less as a succession of stages—which would venture into postulating a consummated finitude of the imaginary by the symbolic—than as the unfolding of the deadlock of being (i.e., forced choice) in repetition; the repetition that alternates, as Dolar formulates it, "the two faces of the drives (as pertaining to the 'I') and desire (as pertaining to the unconscious)"—which are the subject of the enounced and the subject of enunciation (Dolar 2003, 23). In other words, *I do not think* and *I am not* are inseparable provided neither of them (imaginary and symbolic) presents any totality not to end up in its opposite when lurching onto its own gap—the real. Therefore, the problem of subjectivity that calls for a symptom is to be addressed, not as pertaining to each side of the forced choice on its own, rather to the *either-or* that constitutes its dialectical condition (*either* I do not think *or*

I am not), and which is in effect a *neither-nor* when it comes to the possibility of being as such (Dolar 2003, 24).

So what does this add to the course of the drive introduced in Seminar XI—alienation and separation—other than the fact that separation, now, is but a rejection of alienation, and that separation is thus the primordial alienation to separate from (although never completely) through alienation itself (Dolar 2003, 18)? What does Lacan add to the equation here other than that the way to "separation" is henceforth to dive as deep into one's alienation in the Other—that is to say in transference—as required for alienation to symptomatize into something that is neither separation (i.e., imaginary alienation) nor alienation (i.e., symbolic alienation)? This is a step that Dolar formulates in that "faced with our hypothetical villain shouting '*your thought or your being*,' should one cling to thought or to being [that is nonbeing], or else exclaim '*I give up both, only leave me my symptom*'?" (Dolar 2003, 24). However, this "leave me my symptom" opens the question: Is this symptom already there for the subject to be left with, or is what is there not yet a symptom—that is to say that symptom is what id must become? In other words, the question by which the first encounter with an analysand is to unfold—unlike what some traditions derived from Freud's earliest observations thought—is not "what is the symptom?" but "what is not yet a symptom?" It is finally that makes psychoanalysis operate—if one resorts to the most elementary aspect of practice—as, namely, a metapsychology.

Let us return now to the point—in the "October Proposition"—where Lacan starts to sketch out his entry into the endgame, and read his articulation of the subject supposed to know while laying all our focus on the doubling of S1 by the S of transference, which he substantiates by adjoining the Aristotelian notion of particularity to naming—that is to say, by the very properties of S1.

> Let us write in the proper way the supposed of this subject by putting knowledge in its place adjoining the supposition:

$$\frac{\mathrm{S} \quad \xrightarrow{\;\mathrm{S}^{q}\;}}{s\,(\mathrm{S}^{1}, \mathrm{S}^{2}, \ldots.\ \mathrm{S}^{n})}$$

> We recognize on the first line the signifier S of the transference, namely of a subject, with its implication of a signifier that we will call any one whatever [Sq], namely, which supposes only particularity, in Aristotle's sense (always welcome), and thereby supposes yet other things. If it is nameable by a proper noun, it is not because it is distinguished by knowledge, as we shall see. Under the bar, but reduced to the span supposing the first signifier [S1]: the s represents the subject that results from it, implicating in the brackets the knowledge, supposed present, of the signifiers in the unconscious [S2,…. Sn], a signification that takes the place of the still latent referent in this tertiary relationship [S1] which joins it to the signifier-signified couple. We see that if psychoanalysis consists in maintaining an agreed-upon situation between two partners, who pose themselves there as psychoanalysand and psychoanalyst, it can only be developed at the price of the ternary constituent [S1] which is the signifier introduced into the discourse set up by it, the one that has a name [Sq]: the subject supposed to know, a formation, for its part, not of artifice but of inspiration, as detached from the psychoanalysand. (Lacan 2009, 7)

In short, as long as the S^1 that joins signifier to signified, and that alienates by the same token the subject *s* to their junction (constitutive of discourse), is still latent under the signification it produces, the subject supposed to know S^q ensures its representation "as detached from the analysand" (that is to say as extimate), and it is with respect to this representative function that S^q is to be apprehended, first as being a "formation" (i.e., a doubling) and second as ensuring a function of "inspiration" (i.e., a desire). In other words, the subject supposed to know S^q is the doubling of the Other's desire (i.e., lack) present in S^1 as long as it is summoned as the knowledge it generates. Thus, the way forward for analysis is henceforth the scansion of knowledge on the Other's lack in S1 by the medium of its double S^q, the subject supposed to know—scansion being the event in knowledge whereby knowledge is revealed as discourse—that is, in the service of the Other's desire.

Thus, what we are required to apprehend now in the Cartesian cogito, in the flash of wit between the orders of "I do not think" and "I am not," is what occurs in the "I doubt," whose quality of event enunciation cannot manage to reduce to discourse. For after systematically doubting every judgment he could find in his speech, Descartes stumbles on one strange enunciation, he says "I doubt"; yet where he thinks that he doubts, he doubts what he thinks, hence, he doubts being the one thinking that thinking he doubts. So this "I doubt" is neither "I am where I do not think" (for in doubt he is thinking) nor "I think where I am not" (for it is thinking that he doubts). What occurs in the midst of Descartes's assertion of doubt as being his certainty, therefore, is the reversal of the syllogism "either I do not think or I am not" into "neither am I not thinking, nor am I not"—a formula we must preserve at a clear distance from its positivization "I think and I am" that ends up in the meager deduction of "I am in order to think," let alone the thinking thing. In other words, where Descartes says "I doubt," he crystallizes the double negation of being and thinking—which is the negation of both his imaginary and symbolic aphanisis at once—in a single causality, wherefrom he deduces, not "therefore, I am" (i.e., determinate I) as he rushes to assert in his formulation of the cogito, but "therefore, I cannot not be" (i.e., indeterminate subject, that is to say real). What Descartes asserts in his cogito is nothing else than the impossibility of his aphanisis, whether the one that reduces him to thought or the one that annihilates him to counter it.

And here, one cannot but underline Descartes's revival of the apagogic reasoning, accountable for retroacting from the certainty of doubt the symptom of God's desire (i.e., gap), which, resorting to no other logical instance than antithesis, operates rather a scansion than an expansion of signification, thus, what is neither reducible to consciousness nor to knowledge. For, against Wittgenstein's reduction of Cartesian certainty to an absence (rather than a negation) of doubt, on the grounds that what cannot be doubted can lead to no proper assertion (a thesis whose accuracy requires the cogito to function as ostensive reasoning), the axiom that subtends the cogito is "supposing that I could doubt the fact that I doubt, I would still be doubting; therefore, I cannot not be"—a reductio ad absurdum that extracts interpretation from a failing explanation. That is to say that no proper assertion of negativity in retrospect from aphanisis can afford any other path than the very stumbling of aphanisis on the absurd; it is that that Descartes unlocks for us, after all, by abolishing any positive relation to nature as the one withheld in perception-consciousness—the abolishment whereby he extracts from "reality" the Enlightenment's first glimpse of the real. What else would Descartes have qualified in thought of such a divine order, and how would he have brought down the divine otherwise to negativity?

Reduction to the absurd, now, does not only shape Descartes's certainty but any encounter with negativity, the rule of which Freud deposits in "where id was there shall ego be" (Freud 2000–2010, 4687) that Dolar reformulates as "I [as real] was not there" (Dolar 2003, 11). This formula demarcates the very structure of interpretation in psychoanalysis, for what is not strictly negativizing is de facto ego strengthening (a fact overlooked by many psychoanalytic schools) as well as that of the three major theoretical advancements Freud laid as foundation for our praxis. The first of those moments—to revisit them briefly—occurs in Freud's apprenticeship with Charcot, where the successful hypnotic treatment (and even production) of hysteric symptoms points him toward a first dent in both the understanding of hysteria as neurological morbidity and the reductionist empirical standard this understanding aligns with. So Freud's first dent may be formulated as "I (the hysteric's I) was not there in the neuro-logical"—a first account of the failure of modern science to structure its subject. The second of those moments comes in Freud's realization that the hysteric's narrative about incestuous seduction is less accountable as traumatic etiology of symptoms than as phantasmatic formations binding jouissance to the Other's desire—the fulfillment of which (that makes it demand) is attested to in any of the infernal figures of the incestuous. So where Freud abandons his theory of seduction for the Oedipus complex he attests that "I (the hysteric's I) was not there in the Other's demand," that is to say in the imaginary—in "I am where I do not think." And the third moment (the one that is omitted by whoever misses that there is no other Freudianism than Lacanism) comes in Freud's later understanding of the problem of subjectivity as never have been repression but in the failure in repression—that is, the compulsion to repeat wherefrom the drive has finally aligned itself with negation as opposed to the instinct previously sketched out in the life drive. In other words, where Freud announces the death drive as the beyond of the pleasure principle—the latter presenting the binding of satisfaction to discharge—he declares that "I was not there in the symbolic that negativizes jouissance"—in "I think where I am not."

So we are not only compelled to confirm Lorenzo Chiesa's assertion that Descartes was Lacanian well before Lacan—provided the certainty he finds in doubt plays as a scansion of knowledge on the Other's lack—but also that in this very order of things Freud was, properly speaking, a Cartesian, provided the cogitation he turns into praxis aims quite identically at revealing knowledge as being a discourse by the same apagogic reasoning we equated with the event of interpretation (that is scansion), and revealing thereby the Other as being a lack in S^1 (i.e., desire) (Chiesa 2016, 208). This is a point Lacan does not fail to ponder, in spite of the misreading Chiesa underlines. Specifically, Lacan asserts that "Freud's method is Cartesian—in the sense that he sets out from the basis of the subject of certainty" whose sole support is doubt and that, provided the symptom the cogito produces is the subversion of the Other into a gap, what Descartes declares as being an undeceiving Other is to be grasped as rather being undeceived (Lacan 1981, 35–37). Undeceived by what if not by the play of signifiers whose signification summons the subject of enunciation as subject of the enounced? And it is on this particular foundation that Lacan advances now in the "October Proposition" his radicalization of Descartes's method, as the sole necessary condition of analytic praxis that will be henceforth called the desire of the analyst. He writes:

> What matters for us here is the psychoanalyst, in his relation to the knowledge of the supposed subject, not second but direct. It is clear that of the supposed knowledge, he knows nothing. The Sq of the first line has nothing to do with the enchained S's of the second and can only be found there by chance. Let us sharpen this fact to reduce by it the strangeness of the insistence that Freud puts in recommending us to tackle each new case as if we had acquired nothing from its first decipherings. This in no way authorizes the psychoanalyst to have enough with knowing that he knows nothing, for what is at stake, is what he has to get to know about. What he has to know about, can be traced out from the same relationship 'in reserve' according to which all logic worthy of the name operates. This does not mean anything in 'particular,' but is articulated in chains of letters so rigorous that provided not one of them is missed, the not-known is arranged as the framework of knowledge. (Lacan 2009, 8)

So what the analytic function is reducible to is Cartesian doubt in knowledge—"nothing authorizes the psychoanalyst to have enough with knowing that he knows nothing"—whereby the signifiers of the unconscious reveal themselves "by chance"; the chance that Lacan equates elsewhere with *tuché* and thereby repetition. In other words, the analyst's desire for certainty is put into service insofar as it permits, being founded on doubt, repetition to unveil the master signifiers in their synchronic function (i.e., interpretation), rather than their diachronic effect (i.e., signification) (Lacan 1981, 26–54). And it is by this very function that the analyst's desire to know, which is the Cartesian desire for certainty, permits along the lines of synchrony the mapping of the logic of fantasy that traces itself down to its initial term, that is the Other's lack in S^1. In that, the *not-known*—that the subject supposed to know stands for as the double of S^1—which is assigned to the desire of the analyst "is arranged as the framework of knowledge," insofar as what this desire unfolds through the cracks of signification is the measure whereby knowledge may be apprehended as discourse, that is to say desire.

This desire of the analyst is, nevertheless, not to be taken here as the sole business of the analyst; for, let us not forget, it is because transference is impossible that it forms the infinite (i.e., a dialectic), which brings down any prospect of an end of analysis to no more than a *finality*, that is, producing the Cartesian symptom of the analyst's desire in the analysand. This is a point Lacan advances in *On Freud's "Trieb"* in terms of "the rights of a primary aim [*fin première*]" as radically opposed to eschatology (Lacan 2006, 724). In other words, provided that mourning (as in Ferenczi's thesis we examined in the first chapter) warrants no further prospect than the renewal of belief, there can be no better end to analysis than the analyst's desire; the analyst's desire being desire as pure function, which becomes accessible by means of the conviction—to use Freud's term—that it is the Other's desire; that is to say a desire that no longer takes its object cause for jouissance, for it is nothing else than division (Lacan 2006, 724). It is from there that we shall enter next what Lacan calls the endgame to address in it what is properly procedural, the destitution that we shall apprehend now no longer as the opposite of fullness, but that of *restitution*—provided fantasy is but another name for promise.

What Is Not Liquidation Is Not Naming, What Is Not Anarchy Is Not Institution

In order to conclude this work properly, we must depart again from its initial question, the one that Freud poses in "Analysis Terminable and Interminable" about the ambition psychoanalysis may have within the dialectical limit traced by repetition. Yet, if Freud anchors by the end of his trajectory the foundations of the drive in the constancy of repetition, that doesn't make repetition possible in the sense that it ever occurs up to the consummation of its aim. On the contrary, it is because negation is but a failed negation that it has no better prospect than being constantly repeated—a fact this work has addressed through multiple conceptual entries.

What the compulsion to repeat implicates, therefore, is no longer the questioning of some original repressed trauma on whose back anxiety's etiology can be thrown (as in Freud's earlier *neurotica*) but the very necessity whereupon trauma (as aim of the drive) is (insufficiently) produced and reproduced in repetition. This poses, in turn, the question whether trauma may still be conceived as the one there has already been—as diverse psychologies still unite to preach—or the one that is yet to be. What the compulsion to repeat radicalizes once and for all, and to all concerned parties, is that trauma—as an end to division—is what has always not yet occurred, being the supposed final deliverance from the Other's demand, on the one hand, and from the fantasy that objects to it (not without satisfying it), on the other. One must apprehend trauma therefore as being a liberation in whose shade stands the very foundation of alienation—and that, let us not forget, is the subject supposed to know. For what is it that alienates in alienation in the first place if not possibility—to return to Kierkegaard's term—as the trauma whereby alienation may supposedly cease once and for all?

Thus, the question that does justice to repetition is not "why is there that much of repetition?" as the correctionists pose with all their thirst for an end in explanation, but rather: "Why is there not enough of repetition in repetition itself?" "Why does event fail to coin structure?" "Why does event end up event of structure?" On that, let us start by affirming that the position of psychoanalysis is not the one that intends to cease repetition in any way (a point of which "Analysis Terminable and Interminable" constitutes a clear declaration), not even by betting on its consummation in some purgatory of mourning (as sustained by Ferenczi's anti-Freudian theory, which is, ironically, as embraced by Freudian orthodoxy as it is by all the developmentalist renegades who opposed it). What psychoanalysis may afford to claim, in fact, is not a cure but a *farce*; the farce whereby it does credit repetition, yet, precisely against its aim—that is, the fantasmatic deliverance from the Other. For, if psychoanalysis partners with repetition as opposed to therapeutics, it is not to lead it to any fantasized success or consummation but rather to the realization of the very failure in jouissance that makes the condition for division, and thereupon to the apprehension of repetition as being—namely, a repetition of repetition (the Other's in any case).

It is only from there that one may apprehend subjective destitution in consequence with its retroactive value (the traversal of fantasy), provided this traversal gets operated by no other instance than the unveiling of the destitution there is (and there has always been) at the heart of restitution itself—and which derives, in turn, from the fact that one can only afford being, as the *a* the Other lacks, at the price of one's nonbeing. What this entry point offers us in particular is the prospect of weighing destitution—together with the traversal it is formalized into—beyond its common fetishization by the societal mechanisms of analytic institutions. For what subjective destitution stands for is rather less the occurrence of the final event of analysis than the reoccurrence of the initial deadlock of the real that makes it itself divided. One must refer here to analysands' narratives on how, despite the great disruption occurring by their destitution, the state it brings them is far from being unknown—some even manage to describe it by "the most intimate." Subjective destitution must therefore be conceived of rather less as occurrence (i.e., as event) than as reoccurrence (i.e., effect of structure), provided it brings no novelty to the problem of subjectivity other than instating its fundamental limitation, which Frank Ruda formalizes with his claim that *determinism* and *freedom* are one and the same—that is to say that the negation of the forced choice is itself what is mostly forced in it (Ruda 2016, 137).

A path to this procedure—that roots freedom back in determinism—is offered to us in *The Ethics of Psychoanalysis* where, by way of articulating the two deaths involved in the forced choice, Lacan comes to formulate, through a question, a radically new model of their possible relation (Lacan 1992, 295). "Whatever the significance of the metapsychological imagining of Freud's that is the death instinct, whether or not he was justified in forging it, the question it raises is articulated in the following form by virtue of the mere fact that it has been raised: How can man, that is to say a living being, have access to knowledge of the death instinct, to his own relationship to death?" (Lacan 1992, 295). What this formulation of the question answers already is that, if there is a ground on which one can (not transcend but) inhabit the burden of being, that is to say the repetition amid two modalities of nonbeing, it must be the operational relation there is in their conjunction by the drive, and which may, as such, be regarded as a knowledge that demands inscription. The effect of this formulation is groundbreaking, in fact, provided Lacan articulates in what follows it the divided structure of jouissance itself—intertwining Kant's notion of the beautiful and the function of shame—to endorse for the first time in his theoretical trajectory Freud's end to analysis in the terms of a symptom inscribing jouissance in its own lack (Lacan 1992, 295–99). That is, it is out of the incompleteness of the real (Lacan posits here as a knowledge of the drive) necessitating repetition that Freud's running aground on the castration complex can be conceived of as a destitution, insofar as it reveals jouissance and castration as being one and the same. And this is the hypothesis we have chosen to defend in this work, as much against Lacan as on his behalf, up until the advent of this axiom and subsequent declaration. Yet, rather than resting our case, for it still requires that we deal with its political consequences, let us assert that what subjective destitution stands for in its relation to repetition is that it is precisely not *difference* that repeats—as Deleuze declares in his positivizing formula—but "*semblance*," insofar as jouissance is as much a semblance of castration in anxiety than in desire (Lacan 1971, 34).

Would it not render the scale of this crossroad more tangible to recall that it was at its unique site that all scissions took place? The last one, in which "Analysis Terminable and Interminable" resulted in Freud's abandonment by Freudianism itself, is a fate Lacan did not refrain from attempting to reverse by his *dissolution*, which enacted with utmost devotion Freud's return from the dead as "*père-sévère*" to abandon those who turned his discovery against its own ambition (Lacan 2010b, 128). For the battle of psychoanalysis since its very beginnings, and there is no more than one, is that which defends the dialectical rule that makes the scar in the Other—wherefrom derives the stature of a traversal—only affordable by being a scar of the Other. And that does not only involve the fact that the only freedom there is for the speaking subject is itself the crux of alienation, but also that, on those very grounds, this alienation is already a freedom insofar as it is subtended by truth—a point we shall address abundantly a little further in this section.

Should that suffice to disturb the wholesale of destitution, which no longer scares anyone provided lack has already returned in the real, we shall return to the point of the "October Proposition" now where Lacan gives destitution the pivotal function of launching the *endgame* of analysis (Lacan 2009, 11):

> Our purpose is to pose an equation whose constant is the agalma. The psychoanalyst's desire is its enunciating which can operate only from the fact that it comes there in the position of the x: of this very x whose solution delivers to the psychoanalysand his being and whose value is written (- phi) [...]. The structure thus abridged allows you to form an idea of what happens at the end of the transference relation, that is: when the desire that sustained the psychoanalysand in his operation is resolved, he no longer wants at the end to take up its option, that is the remainder which as the determinant of his division, makes it fall from his phantasy and destitutes him as subject. (Lacan 2009, 10)

In other words, insofar as the analyst's desire delivers the jouissance it had inscribed back to the subject in its (retroactively) original form, which is not the missed jouissance that remains a negation of (*- phi*), but the missing jouissance (*- phi*) that results from the doubling of its negation, the subject's desire for analysis (i.e., for the analyst's desire) gets resolved. But what does it get resolved by? By the "fall," Lacan tells us, not *of fantasy* as many have deduced from those lines, but of the "remainder" that the analyst's desire inscribed "from fantasy." What is crucial to discern here is that this resolution conjectures, not the disavowal of fantasy as such, but that of the positivized jouissance it promised; which plays, in turn, as an admittance of fantasy's inevitability, provided what gets asserted amid destitution is that fantasy presents not a mean to jouissance in itself, but is, as such, jouissance for itself. That is to say that fantasy is the only jouissance there can be, which entails that jouissance as such is what of fantasy gets traversed. Such is the formalization we owe to the analysand who abandon their regular sessions on the conviction that whatever it is that they desire—now that analysis has revealed enough of it—it will always remain a fantasy.

Away, therefore, from whoever bargains out of those lines the prospect of a life beyond fantasy (whether one calls that an *analyst* or not), the fact analysis can afford to claim is that the "change of tack" it involves establishes not the guarantee (which, let us not forget, is the subject supposed to know) of disentangling being from structure in some beyond of fantasy (i.e., fantasy itself) but the guarantee there is in the very failure of that guarantee (Lacan 2009, 13). Must one recall here how, owing to the fact that the neurotic no longer "imagines [by the end of their analysis] he is a pervert" (the only one whose fantasy succeeds), what comes out of the neurotic's analysis is neurosis itself (Lacan 2006, 699)? This is a point that must be accepted if one cares to curb the revival of fantasy by the very idea of its traversal; for, what of fantasy may be strictly traversed is that it may successfully lead to a positive jouissance.

Yet, what unfolds out of this axiom requires even more caution, for not only does it delimit for us the domain of a concept of finality for analysis but it also pinpoints its very internal crack and engages with it incisively by the necessity of the pass—a theoretical ambition that only belief would exchange for the liberal ideal of *transmission* of psychoanalysis. Where Lacan locates this crack—which attests once more that the object of psychoanalysis is not the object *a*, but the very dialectic the *a* derives from—is in the fact that, with respect to the dialectical limit drawn by destitution (that jouissance is but a semblance of castration), nothing resolves the analyst's desire other than *the desire of the analyst*—the point we have previously addressed in that there is no analysis that is not de facto didactic. Lacan writes: "The true original [analysis] can only be the second, by constituting the repetition that makes the first into an act, for this is what introduces into it the after effect proper to logical time, which is marked by the fact that the psychoanalysand has become a psychoanalyst" (Lacan 2009, 12). This is a crack we must open as wide as the concept demands, despite whatever difficulties (or discontent) that might cause to psychoanalytic ideologies: if nothing resolves the analyst's desire other than the desire of the analyst, then no analysis has ever ended without a pass—whether one utters in that pass what Lacan called for in this "October Proposition," or the one by which Descartes injected negativity into the comfort of Jesuit supremacy (Lacan 2009, 12–13). The point here, should one care for preserving the Lacanian ambition, is to seek in whatever has produced a symptom the order of pass (and thus, the analytic act) there is already, rather than discrediting whichever analysis that hasn't undergone a formal pass—for such kind of rigor has nothing more to offer than the religious. Is it not Lacan's position after all that "analysis is, in sum, the reduction of initiation [...] to the fact that strictly speaking there is no initiation" at the point where he introduces the work of James Joyce as an accurate analytic trajectory on the grounds that the literary pass it produced was sufficient in result (Lacan 2016, 20–147)?

That "no analysis afford to be what it claims without a *passe*" is nevertheless not without consequences. Not only does it mean that production can only be questioned in retrospect from the order it reforms, "(not what is, but) what was analysis?" (be that what causes antiphilosophy as much trouble with psychoanalysis than that which it already has with philosophy). It also means that "the logics of traversal and of testimony," as Gabriel Tupinambá divides them, are inseparable, provided a traversal (if one does not hold onto the liquidation of transference) only becomes traversal when it gets formalized in a testimony—that is, the symptom in knowledge that founds the analytic act (Tupinambá 2021, 193–204). And that is the case insofar as testimony is what allows a traversal for itself where its ontological limitation prevents it from being in itself. Is that not the fundamental insufficiency that distinguishes the result of psychoanalysis from the effect of therapeutics (only to promise such a thing as a liquidation) and that makes it end on nothing else than its very beginning as initiation? That is why no thematic rupture enables us in this "Proposition" to locate Lacan's move from formalizing the traversal to structuring the testimony; what he offers us instead is a working through of traversal as already being a testimony, with the sole difference of logical time (Lacan 2009, 4). That is to say that it is from the logical point of testimony that destitution may be formalized as a traversal. Lacan writes:

> Let him [the former analysand] know from what I [the henceforth analyst] did not know [as analysand] about the being of desire [as the *désêtre* brought by destitution], how things stand with him, having come to the being of knowledge [by testimony], and let him [the former analysand] efface himself [into an analyst].' *Sicut palea*, as St. Thomas said of his work at the end of his life, like manure. In this way the being of desire [*désêtre*] rejoins the being of knowledge [the subject supposed to know] in order to be reborn from it by their being knotted in a strip with a single edge on which a single lack is inscribed, the one that sustains [by the desire of the analyst] the agalma [formerly inscribed in the analyst's desire]. (Lacan 2009, 13)

So if it is traversal that resolves the analyst's desire by the desire of the analyst ("the lack that sustains the agalma"), it can only be afforded by the testimony which knots together the *désêtre* revealed by destitution as "being of desire" and "the being of knowledge" (i.e., the subject supposed to know). This knotting, nevertheless, exceeds knotting provided what comes out of it is "a single lack," Lacan tells us, wherein neither does jouissance (once unveiled as *désêtre*) get to sustain castration as complex, nor does castration (once exposed beyond the complex as) being the Other's get to positivize jouissance in him. In other words, this *single lack* is the inscription of jouissance as semblance of castration beyond the complex—a point I already addressed in the third chapter as a *rescuing of castration*—from which its very status is shifted from impotence to impossibility.

But what is it exactly that allows this inscription? It is "not simply a process of negation," Tupinambá claims, "but a process of naming at the point of negation" that gives otherness a "perimeter and situated determination," as "the passage [Lacan states in the *Proposition*] from the potential infinity of natural numbers to the first transfinite number"(Lacan 2009, 8; Tupinambá 2021, 201). Yet, why would one consider a transfinite number a naming when it functions precisely as a sign? And what does calling that a naming entail, other than affirming the derivability of an immediate traversal of fantasy from subjective destitution—that is to say a liquidation of transference—without the mediacy of a testimony that forms a symptom by producing a concept? This is a line that Tupinambá sustains, in fact, not without underlining in it the limitation in naming that would still call for a pass (and thus a concept); yet, always from the outset of his splitting between traversal and testimony (Tupinambá 2021, 201–2). This leaves us pray to the revival—by the theory of naming—of the therapeutic aim of liquidation, and with it, the reduction of the traversal of fantasy to the promise of its very preservation. For what is fantasy in the first place if not the very idea that fantasy may be traversed?

Moreover, what this confronts us with is the question whether the axiom Tupinambá appoints further to the pass really complements what supposedly gets started in naming, or whether it rather dismantles it (Tupinambá 2021, 204). For how would an axiom—that brings the real into knowledge by antithesis—align itself with naming when it is unnaming that it operates for synthesis to occur? This is a point that Todd McGowan touches upon in his reading of Hegel's *Science of Logic* by designating as concept the encounter of thought with the contradiction in knowledge that reveals the contradiction in being—which Hegel qualifies as "reason's [...] ability to think the contradiction that inhabits all being, to articulate how being necessarily involves its own negation" (McGowan 2019, 198). On that, inasmuch as it is contradiction that an axiom reveals, which entails reducing the authority the name sustains by noncontradiction through its inscription in the opposition that renders it signifier, what an axiom is to operate for it to have been a concept is not a naming but an unnaming (McGowan 2019, 198). This is a line of thought that Tupinambá does not avoid pondering and opposing on the grounds that what it advances against the theory of naming is that "the operation which leads us from transference to the traversal is qualitatively distinct from the one ruling over the sequential logic of signification" (Tupinambá 2021, 203). This is a categorization one cannot oppose any less than its preceding in fact, for traversal is not conceivable as a beyond of transference (provided that is precisely what would negate it as traversal) and the axiom (that by unnaming will have been a concept) is also not conceivable as being "distinct from the sequential logic of signification," provided it is by its very retroactive function that the sequence subtending signification is revealed as discourse and reversed.

One must also signal here that any wager that situates the outlook of analysis under *naming* necessarily falls into the pre-Cartesian foundation—which structuralism modernized—that throws the matter on the impotence of perception because it situates its deadlock rather in the unnamed than the named. This is a wager that no psychoanalytic thinking can afford to sustain any further, given that it negates the unconscious by the very means of articulating its consequence. Moreover, what we have here is a matter that Freud settled on clear Cartesian foundations, insofar as "Wo Es war, soll Ich warden" precisely states—"where it was just now, [...] I can [*peut*] come into being by disappearing from my statement [*dit*]"—that if analysis attributes any value to naming, it is strictly within the measure that, by naming, unnaming can occur (Lacan 2006, 678). This compels us to affirm that what may properly turn subjective destitution into a traversal of fantasy is neither "negation" nor "naming at the point of negation" but quite the reverse: the axiom that unnames lack and restricts it from getting named ever again—and that is the function of testimony. For what else than such an axiom can restrict agalma's negativity from reigniting dogma, at the point where it is precisely out of dogma that it is supposed to slip, in its pass from the analyst's desire to the desire of the analyst?

This is a point Oedipus—the outcast—defended with equal misery to that which leads an analysand to their testimony, not only by his insisting plea, "I am not guilty," but mostly by the subversion of this plea—as Zupančič tells us—into the judgment of the very law whereby his act was being judged, "if only I were guilty!" (Zupančič 2000, 178–95). What does Oedipus claim here if not that the instance that names his act misses it by its very naming, and that—having settled his dues by continuing his life as an outcast rather than heroically ending it—it was owed to him that lack goes unnamed (i.e., unpositivized)? "If only I were 'guilty,' my act would have been 'enjoyment,' and my desire would have been mine; but since it was not I who desired—which I nevertheless paid for as if I did—the Other shall name it no more" (Zupančič 2000, 186). In that, "Oedipus does not identify with his destiny," Zupančič explains, "he identifies [...] with that thing in him which made possible the realization of this destiny: he identifies with his blindness" (Zupančič 2000, 179). This implies that what Oedipus truly defended by resisting naming is the symptom—"if I were guilty, I would not have been blind"—whereby he inscribed lack in the Other and disabled him from positivizing it any further, which he ensured by answering the chorus by the inverse of its demand (Zupančič 2000, 179). What does this ending of tragedy on the tragic emphasize, if not the eternal opposition of the symptom to the name? And what does Oedipus declare here other than that he would only have been if the matter does not get settled or liquidated? So, rather than a name that indefinitely necessitates a symptom, he opts for a symptom that unnames indefinitely; a sufficient indication that nothing must come out of the forced choice other than the forced choice itself; that is to say, no liquidation—that is, naming—whatsoever can afford to be what it claims.

But does that spare us the burden of questioning what the singularity of the testimony that ends the analysand's destitution is made of, when analysis altogether—and destitution with it—is one long wrecked testimony? And what is it that is not already a testimony in the order that, not only neutralizes testimony by the same legislation that permits it but also commands it insofar as it ensures opinion, which by itself endorses the discourse of the master as much by belief (the university discourse) as by complaint (the hysteric's discourse)—let alone the eternal dream of overthrow that preaches the better master only to end up bringing out the worst (Lacan 1971, 43; Chiesa 2016, 148). Our question becomes, therefore, what is it in the order of testimonies that is not an opinion? In other words, what discourse is it that might not be a semblance? This is a question that no historicizing narrative about one's analysis can suffice to answer, for what is required from testimony for testimony not to be a semblance is the cut through this narrative onto the dialectic that delimits, as destitution, what is and has been the actual all along. It is there, in fact, that one grasps the theory of the four discourses as a necessary axiom in the reasoning that unfolds from the question of the finality of analysis, once its political magnitude is restored (what, if anything, is revolution?) by the evidence that no subjective destitution was ever surpassed (i.e., became a traversal) without a testimony. For why would one speak to a *passeur*, or passer, about one's destitution if one was not still in it? This is a fact that is evidenced enough by the length of the period over which the exchange with a passer used to be spread, as by the fact that, in most cases, this exchange started while analytic sessions were still ongoing.

Now, if semblance is “entirely a fact of discourse,” that is to say an artifact, what might not be a semblance, according to Lacan, is the “discourse which […] posits that the discourse […] is a semblance” (Lacan 1971, 25–33). A claim one must situate in direct sequence with the Cartesian cogito, insofar as it aims at rescuing methodological doubt from its obfuscation by the discourse of science. For what this adds to the Cartesian methodology is that, for doubt to pave the path to certainty, it cannot content itself with scrutinizing prior judgments as knowledge by the medium of formal logic but must also scrutinize these judgments as effect of the real, that is to say as discourse, and amend formal logic with the logic through which discourse had been subtended by truth (Chiesa 2016, 82). One mustn't confuse this axiom with the situation of analysis in the domain of science (as that of science which treats the problem of truth), for this axiom is far more brutal in fact; what Lacan advances here is that, provided formal logic does not save modern science from being a discourse, modern science cannot claim to be *science* without psychoanalysis—if not the project of the Enlightenment which analysis revived from within the failure of science in structuring its subject.

Thus, if the discourse that might not be a semblance is—as discourse of the analyst—that which amends the logic that determines error by the one which determines the determination of error by truth—which makes it the obverse side of the discourse of the master, it is not enough to say it is a discourse that advances formalization; for, of all formalizations, it is the one that formalizes what in formalization is unformalizable, allowing formalization thereby to address problems which would have otherwise remained inaccessible to it (Chiesa 2016, 148). Thus, the discourse of the analyst is that which inscribes the nonformal—that is, the exception to the formal that makes formal the law of knowledge—in the formal itself, an operation that Lacan condenses in the controverting term (the analyst's) knowledge of truth (Chiesa 2016, 149). However, this knowledge of truth requires that language surpass its semblance by becoming writing, Chiesa tells us, since in writing, “‘something […of language] is found not to be simply a representation,’ in the sense that it is at the same time a 'repercussion' on speech, an 'event of discourse' through which the subject [...] interrogates the very way in which discourse manages to master itself" (Chiesa 2016, 84). Is that not what is aimed at, after all, where Oedipus moans "if only I were guilty!" to reaffirm his blindness? For this blindness that takes the function of a writing, "in logically interrogating the incompleteness of language, is not language—since it could be language here only as meta-language," that is to say as a positivization of the incompleteness of language (Chiesa 2016, 86). And that amounts to "the fact that *l'achose* cannot be said, yet can be demonstrated" (Chiesa 2016, 86).

It is from there that we shall affirm now that what of the analysand's speech may be called a testimony is that which advances the axiom whereby the incompleteness of language gets rather demonstrated than named, and that produces a writing, thus, whose function is that of the symptom that restricts its further naming. The question that testimony confronts us with, therefore, is not simply "what does an analysand's transference become after analysis?"—a formulation that reduces the matter to technicity. Rather the question is "what order does psychoanalysis establish as law?" This is a political ambition Lacan makes sure to end his "Proposition" on, by defying what he calls the three *facticities* not of the institution (for we shall not buy that institution is itself what institutes) but of the instituted by science—which are the family of the petit bourgeois, the unit as Freud designates by it the army and the church, and the concentration camp, which in our epoch is that of mass media; that is to say that we are already all in it (Lacan 2009, 16–17). But what does Lacan defy the instituted with? It is neither the creation of the pass as a procedure (for it had been discussed in writing long before having this name) nor its institutionalization (for it is what goes precisely against the instituted). Rather, what Lacan defies the instituted with is the staging of the pass as the experiment of submitting authority (the jury of agreement) to the trial that purifies it from fiction—that is to say from the discourse of the master.

> What the style and the ends of this organization owe to the blackout imposed on the function of the didactic analysis, is obvious as soon as a look at them is allowed: hence the isolation with which it protects itself.

> The objections that our proposal has encountered, does not stem in our School from such an organic fear. The fact that they are expressed in a justifiable theme already mobilises self-criticism. The verification of ability, calling for fairer titles, is no longer ineffable. It is by such a trial that authority makes itself recognized. Let the assembly of technicians know that it is not a question of contesting authority, but of removing it from fiction. (Lacan 2009, 18)

What does that tell us other than that the true authority—that is to say the authority of truth—is not that of the master (the fiction) but that of its obverse side? In other words, wherever the didactic title is summoned as some proof of mastery, there is rather too little ambition rather than too much; provided the standpoint of psychoanalysis is not the one whose purpose is getting recognized by the master as science but the exact reverse, the one that aims no lower than turning his science against him—that is, rescuing the slave's labor from its annihilation in the master's knowledge (Lacan 1971, 34).

We can no longer settle, thus, for the maneuver by which the pass had been sold as a modality of recruiting analysts, a maneuver whose necessity was verified enough, in any case, by the troubles it brought to Lacan's followers. Buying that would only blind us to what really occurs underneath the prestigious appellation of jury of agreement, and which constitutes the true weight of this procedure. For as Tupinambá underlines, a jury of agreement that is consequent with its name would only guarantee another "hierarchy of recognition," which would cause in turn—as far as this can be from a pass—the usual naming of analysts based on their order of descendance as done in any psychoanalytic institution that calls itself quite rightly a *society* (Tupinambá 2021, 211). Nevertheless, what of this organization may be regarded as a guarantor of a pass, Tupinambá tells us, is "the invariant idea" that this jury of agreement is meant to find across the testimonies of three different passers accompanying a single *passant*, and which is supposed to constitute in itself a "proposition of a new problem," that is to say a gap in the psychoanalytic knowledge that preceded it—this is the axiom that renders the passant's speech a testimony (Tupinambá 2021, 211–12). What this jury of agreement is supposed to agree on, therefore, is nothing else than the gap that a passant produces in the knowledge it speaks. This implicates that neither is the jury a jury, for it is its very knowledge that is being scrutinized, nor is the passant a passant—for it is the passant who scrutinizes it. The bottom line is that no pass worthy of the name has ever been a pass of the analysand who undergoes it, rather that of the analyst as such if not that of psychoanalysis altogether. What else does such a procedure declare than that psychoanalysis survives not by *transmission*—which is the case of what is instituted by science—but by *discontinuity* and *reinvention*?

Should we not designate here the drift there is in making such an experiment stand as institution, and an institution that, to twist the knife in the wound, is proud to proclaim the transmission of psychoanalysis? What the pass sides with, in fact, is rather an ever-renewed constitution than institution, provided the gap it operates in structure rather occurs by discontinuity than transmission. This is an axiom Lacan establishes his "Italian Note" on when, after five troublesome years of submitting the *Ecole* to this trial, he went as far as suggesting to his Italian counterparts that they should found no more of the institution than its very gap, even at the risk of ending up with no psychanalytic group at all (Lacan 2010b, 1–3). Does that not sufficiently state one needn't add to the instituted, which is, there is no other, the instituted by science, but subtract from it? This is a point that confronts us again to the great burden of the left, whose misadventures were as many in the dogmatic institution as in anarchy—the latter being, as Lacan underlines in the "events" of 1968, not the opposite of institution but its absoluteness (Rabaté 2009, 38). Is there any novelty therefore in the idea that the *will to power*, whether it calls itself an institution or an anarchy, is never distinct (as long as alienation gets not summoned as oppression) from the logic against which it revolts? It is against this very obedience to science (as the master's knowledge) in both of those facticities that Lacan ends his "Italian Note" by expecting from his recruits the quality of *stubbornness* to go beyond the means of formal logic—"find me an analyst of this stubbornness (*tuile*), who will plug the yoke into something other than a roughly sketched-out organon" (Lacan 2010b, 1–3). This is a demand one finds being repeated in the *Letter of Dissolution*, as Lacan recruits out of the *Ecole* at the moment of dissolving it, those of its members who can commit to the "'assiduous criticism' [... of its] 'deviations, and compromises' [...]

demonstrating through acts that it is not of their doing that [… it] would be an Institution" (Lacan 2010b, 129).

It is from this point that we shall finally return to Tupinambá's thesis on the aftermath of transference, which spares us indeed the trouble of a liquidated transference—for he speaks of a "return to transference […] without an analyst," yet, not without conserving that of the analytic institution—for he makes "the institution of psychoanalysis as such fill this role" (Tupinambá 2021, 207). Tupinambá summarizes this thesis a little further in the following terms:

> The logic of the testimony […] returns to the inconsistency of the Other through a recourse to formal consistency […] it addresses itself not to the analyst, but to the passers, who both numerically and as mediators, conform a new form of otherness that places the psychoanalytic institution as the testimony's address; and […] it substitutes the suture of the subject (transference) and the subjective destitution (traversal) for the nonsubjective subject of the analytic formalism itself. (Tupinambá 2021, 207)

Despite the accuracy this formulation offers in terms of designating what analysis there is after analysis, that is to say the transference there is as aftermath of transference, it still requires that we engage with a set of political problems it raises. First, although it is clear that the subject of the signifier—which is revealed itself as being *désêtre*—is yielded, as of the moment of the pass, in a "subject of the analytic formalism," nothing permits us from conceiving this subject of formalism as exceeding transference, provided it is nothing else than transference, that is to say discourse and its semblance, that in formalism it treats. In other words, were it not for the insistence of transference beyond analysis, neither analytic formalism nor its subject would be necessary; the subject of formalism is, therefore, only distinct from the subject of the signifier by means of methodology, otherwise they are one and the same. Second, the fact that the "authentication" of a pass lies in the sole condition that the passer must be in a pass themself—that is to say at the end of their analysis—states already the requirement that they not confuse their function with that of the passant's addressee—neither "numerically" nor as "mediator," provided the passer is supposed to authenticate the passant's axiom only if it works for them as passant (Lacan 2009, 14). In that, the passer is rather a partner than an addressee in the project of amending the function of addressee as such. And third, inasmuch as the axiom produced by the collaboration of two passants—for this is how they are designated when one does not limit the pass to some will to be recognized as analyst—is meant to amend (i.e., interpret) the psychoanalytic knowledge of the jury under its own agreement, it is rather the passant that is the addressee of knowledge than the jury (Lacan 2009, 15). So the psychoanalytic knowledge that is instituted is on the opposite side of this *addressee* who is the passant—for what are they designated as analyst of, after all, if not the school (Lacan 2009, 2)? It is also a matter of reverting this knowledge (i.e., discourse of the master) into a discourse of the analyst that is entirely handed to them.

So there is not a valid necessity to conserve the idea of analytic institution as a beyond of the liquidation of transference—provided the beyond of one is already the beyond of all. And there is also not a sufficient reason not to acknowledge in the passer (in line with, but not limited to, the passer's designation by this "Proposition") an established political category that replaces that of the analyst in their discursive function—for no analysis is ever ended before the analyst is unveiled, in fact, as having been a passer all along, and a passant. What else than in having been no more than a passer does the analyst dispense the subject supposed to know into exchange? Moreover, if "a madman is [...] an analyst who thinks he is an analyst," as Žižek writes in the foreword to Tupinambá's *The Desire of Psychoanalysis*, an analyst who only assumes to *have been* an analyst in the measure that the imposture of "being an analyst" was required by the function of passer is not a madman (Tupinambá 2021, xii). That is to say that passer is the analyst's function beyond the analytic imposture, insomuch as discourse passes through it from the discourse of the master to that of the analyst.

What else was there in the "Letter of Dissolution," after all, than the fierce defense of the function of passer? For when one reads this letter closely, that is to say as *père-sévérance* of the "October Proposition," one finds in it Lacan's correction to Freud's abandoning of his Wednesday's Psychological Society (which functioned almost as a pass) for the international unit that realigned psychoanalysis with the discourse of science—a decision whose historical necessity it has satisfied enough to end up as useless (Lacan 2009, 3). "If I persevere [*père-sévère:* severe-father], it is because the experiment completed calls for a compensatory counter-experiment. I don't need many. And there are many whom I don't need. I am abandoning them here so that they may show me what they can do, aside from burden me and turn to water a teaching in which everything has been carefully weighed" (Lacan 2010b, 129). Should one stress any further how Lacan attempts here to abandon the many for the few where Freud had abandoned the few for many? And what for, if not that "the experiment completed calls for a compensatory counter-experiment"—that is, for the fact that destitution is traversal only if there has been a pass? How can one miss the fact that psychoanalysis as a political project knows no other foundation than the passer, whose function neither warrants anarchy nor institution, but their very interpretation as figures of the same fiction? This is how analysis contributes to the question of revolution, in designating as revolution the one there has been in what was written about revolution, rather than that which from this writing was supposed (by the instituted) to result—a point George Orwell whispers to us in that "every revolutionary opinion draws part of its strength from a secret conviction that nothing can be changed" (Orwell 2020, 101). This does not entail that this book will end on the idea that revolution must be permanent, but that it has already been; such is the difference between an analyst taken for a passer and a passer taken for an analyst, the latter leaves no other stain than dialectics.

Note

1. With reference to the *Letter of Dissolution*.

References

Balmès, François. 2011. L'aliénation et le désir de l'analyste. *Scripta*: 137–62.
Chiesa, Lorenzo. 2016. *The Not-Two: Logic and God in Lacan*. Cambridge, MA: MIT Press.

Dolar, Mladen. 2003. Cogito as the Subject of the Unconscious. In *Critical Evaluation in Cultural Theory*, ed. Jacques Lacan, vol. 2. London: Routledge.

———. 2018. *Best Not To Be Born*. London: EGS, June 20.

Freud, Sigmund. 2000–2010. New Introductory Lectures on Psycho-Analysis (1916–17). In *Freud: Complete Works*, translated and edited by Ivan Smith. https://www.valas.fr/IMG/pdf/Freud_Complete_Works.pdf.

Gueroult, Martial. 1952/1984. *Descartes's Philosophy Interpreted According to the Order of Reasons*. Vol. 2. Translated by Roger Ariew and Alan Donagan. Minneapolis: The University of Minnesota Press.

Lacan, Jacques. 1971. On a Discourse that Might not be a Semblance. The Seminar of Jacques Lacan, vol. XVIII. Translated by Cormac Gallagher. *Lacan in Ireland* (blog). http://www.lacaninireland.com/web/wp-content/uploads/2010/06/THE-SEMINAR-OF-JACQUES-LACAN-XVIII.pdf

———. 1964/1981. *The Four Fundamental Concepts of Psycho-analysis*. The Seminar of Jacques Lacan, vol. XI. Edited by Jacques-Alain Miller and translated by Alan Sheridan. New York: W. W. Norton.

———. 1992. *The Ethics of Psychoanalysis, 1959–1960*. The Seminar of Jacques Lacan, vol. VII. Edited by Jacques-Alain Miller and translated by Dennis Porter. New York: W. W. Norton.

———. 2006. *Ecrits: The First Complete Edition in English*. Edited and translated by Bruce Fink. New York: W. W. Norton.

———. 2009. Proposal of 9 October 1967 on the Psychoanalyst of the School, Second Draft. Translated by Cormac Gallagher. *Lacan in Ireland* (blog), http://www.lacaninireland.com/web/wp-content/uploads/2010/06/Proposal-of-the-analyst-of-the-school-1967.pdf.

———. 2010b. The Logic of Phantasy 1966–1967. The Seminar of Jacques Lacan, vol. XIV. Translated by Cormac Gallagher from unedited French manuscripts. Lacan in Ireland (blog), http://www.lacaninireland.com/web/wpcontent/uploads/2010/06/THE-SEMINAR-OF-JACQUES-LACAN-XIV.pdf.

———. 2011. Transference 1960–1961. The Seminar of Jacques Lacan, vol. VIII. Translated by Cormac Gallagher. Lacan in Ireland (blog). http://hdl.handle.net/10788/158.

———. 2016. *The Sinthome 1975–1976*. The Seminar of Jacques Lacan, vol. XXIII. Edited by Jacques-Alain Miller and translated by A. R. Price. Cambridge: Polity Press.

McGowan, Todd. 2019. *Emancipation After Hegel*. New York: Columbia University Press.

Orwell, George. 2020. *The Road to Wigan Pier*. Oxford: Oxford University Press.
Rabaté, Jean-Michel. 2009. 68+ 1: Lacan's année érotique. *Parrhesia* 6: 28–45.
Ruda, Frank. 2016. *Abolishing Freedom: A Plea for a Contemporary Use of Fatalism*. Lincoln: University of Nebraska Press.
Schuster, Aaron. 2017. Impossible Professions, and How to Defend Them. In *Homestead of Dilution*, ed. Domenico Mangano, Marieke van Rooy, and Niekolaas Johannes Lekkerkerk. Eindhoven: Onomatopee.
Tupinambá, Gabriel. 2021. *The Desire of Psychoanalysis: Exercises in Lacanian Thinking*. Evanston: Northwestern University Press.
Zupančič, Alenka. 2000. *Ethics of the Real: Kant, Lacan*. London: Verso.

References

Unless otherwise noted, all translations of these works are my own.

Avello, José Jiménez. 2000. La métapsychologie chez Ferenczi. Pulsion de mort ou passion de mort? *Le Coq-Héron, Ferenczi et la psychanalyse contemporaine* 154: 17–25.

Azouri, Chawki. 2015. *J'ai réussi là où le paranoïaque échoue*. Toulouse: Erès.

Balmès, François. 2011. L'aliénation et le désir de l'analyste. *Scripta*: 137–62.

Brassier, Ray. 2019. Strange Sameness: Hegel, Marx and the Logic of Estrangement. *Angelaki* 24 (1): 98–105.

Chiesa, Lorenzo. 2016. *The Not-Two: Logic and God in Lacan*. Cambridge, MA: MIT Press.

Claudel, Paul. 2016. The Way of the Cross (1867–1955). Translated by John Dunaway. *Logos* 19 (2, Spring): 177–186.

Comay, Rebecca, and Frank Ruda. 2018. *The Dash: The Other Side of Absolute Knowing*. Cambridge, MA: MIT Press.

Dolar, Mladen. 2003. Cogito as the Subject of the Unconscious. In *Critical Evaluation in Cultural Theory*, ed. Jacques Lacan, vol. 2. London: Routledge.

———. 2005. Nothing Has Changed. *Filozofski Vestnik* 26 (2): 147–160.

———. 2017. Being and MacGuffin. *Crisis and Critique* 4: 1.

———. 2018. *Best Not To Be Born*. London: EGS, June 20.

Dor, Joël. 2001. *Structure and Perversions*. New York: Other Press.

Durkheim, Emile. 1915. *The Elementary Forms of the Religious Life*. Translated by Joseph Ward Swain. London: George Allen and Unwin.

M. Tal, *The End of Analysis*, The Palgrave Lacan Series,
https://doi.org/10.1007/978-3-031-29889-9

Ferenczi, Sándor. 1938. *Thalassa: A Theory of Genitality*, 372–374. Translated by Henry Bunker. The Psychoanalytic Quarterly.

———. 1982. Le Problème de La Fin de L'Analyse. In *Psychanalyse IV. Œuvres Complètes 1927–1933*. Payot.

———. 1985a. Destin des Enfants de Malades Mentaux. *Journal clinique:(janvier-octobre 1932)*: 134–136.

———. 1985b. Projection de la Psychologie des Adultes sur les Enfants. *Journal clinique, (janvier–octobre 1932)*. Payot.

Freud, Sigmund. 1964. Analysis Terminable and Interminable. In *Moses and Monotheism, An Outline of Psycho-Analysis, and Other Works*, vol. 23 of The Standard Edition of the Complete Psychological Works of Sigmund Freud. Translated by James Strachey. London: Hogarth Press.

———. 2000–2010a. Five Lectures on Psycho-Analysis. (1909). In *Freud: Complete Works*, translated and edited by Ivan Smith. https://www.valas.fr/IMG/pdf/Freud_Complete_Works.pdf.

———. 2000–2010b. From the History of an Infantile Neurosis, (1918). In *Freud: Complete Works*, translated and edited by Ivan Smith. https://www.valas.fr/IMG/pdf/Freud_Complete_Works.pdf.

———. 2000–2010c. A Seventeenth-Century Demonological Neurosis. (1923). In *Freud: Complete Works*, translated and edited by Ivan Smith. 2000, 2007, 2010. https://www.valas.fr/IMG/pdf/Freud_Complete_Works.pdf.

———. 2000–2010d. Some Psychical Consequences of the Anatomical Distinction Between the Sexes (1925). In *Freud: Complete Works*, translated and edited by Ivan Smith. https://www.valas.fr/IMG/pdf/Freud_Complete_Works.pdf.

———. 2000–2010e. An Outline of Psycho-Analysis (1940). In *Freud: Complete Works*, translated and edited by Ivan Smith. https://www.valas.fr/IMG/pdf/Freud_Complete_Works.pdf.

———. 2000–2010f. Splitting of the Ego in the Process of Defence (1940). In *Freud: Complete Works*, translated and edited by Ivan Smith. https://www.valas.fr/IMG/pdf/Freud_Complete_Works.pdf.

———. 2000–2010g. New Introductory Lectures on Psycho-Analysis (1916–17). In *Freud: Complete Works*, translated and edited by Ivan Smith. https://www.valas.fr/IMG/pdf/Freud_Complete_Works.pdf.

Granoff, Wladimir. 1958. Ferenczi: faux problème ou vrai malentendu. *Psychanalyse* 6: 255–282.

Gueroult, Martial. 1984. *Descartes's Philosophy Interpreted According to the Order of Reasons*. Vol. 2. Translated by Roger Ariew and Alan Donagan. Minneapolis: The University of Minnesota Press.

Gutiérrez-Peláez, Miguel. 2015. Ferenczi's Anticipation of the Traumatic Dimension of Language: A Meeting with Lacan. *Contemporary Psychoanalysis* 51 (1): 137–154.

Harari, Roberto. 2001. *Lacan's Seminar on "Anxiety": An Introduction"*. Cambridge: Other Press.

Hegel, Georg Wilhelm Fredrich. 2018. *The Phenomenology of Spirit.* Translated by Terry Pinkard and Michael Baur. Cambridge: Cambridge University Press.

Josephus, Flavius. 1737. The Antiquities of the Jews. In *The Complete Works of Flavius Josephus*. Translated by William Whiston. https://archive.org/details/CompleteWorksOfJosephusTranslatedByWilliamWhiston1737.

Kierkegaard, Søren. 1957. *The Concept of Dread.* Translated by Walter Lowrie. Princeton: Princeton University Press.

Lacan, Jacques. 1971. On a Discourse that Might not be a Semblance. The Seminar of Jacques Lacan, vol. XVIII. Translated by Cormac Gallagher. *Lacan in Ireland* (blog). http://www.lacaninireland.com/web/wp-content/uploads/2010/06/THE-SEMINAR-OF-JACQUES-LACAN-XVIII.pdf

———. 1981. *The Four Fundamental Concepts of Psycho-analysis.* The Seminar of Jacques Lacan, vol. XI. Edited by Jacques-Alain Miller and translated by Alan Sheridan. New York: W. W. Norton.

———. 1987. *Letter to D. W. Winnicott.* Translated by J. M. Mehlman. *October* 40.

———. 1992. *The Ethics of Psychoanalysis, 1959–1960.* The Seminar of Jacques Lacan, vol. VII. Edited by Jacques-Alain Miller and translated by Dennis Porter. New York: W. W. Norton.

———. 2006. *Ecrits: The First Complete Edition in English.* Edited and translated by Bruce Fink. New York: W. W. Norton.

———. 2007. *The Other Side of Psychoanalysis.* The Seminar of Jacques Lacan, Vol. XVII. Edited by Jacques-Alain Miller, Translated by Russel Grigg. New York: W. W. Norton.

———. 2009. Proposal of 9 October 1967 on the Psychoanalyst of the School, Second Draft. Translated by Cormac Gallagher. *Lacan in Ireland* (blog), http://www.lacaninireland.com/web/wp-content/uploads/2010/06/Proposal-of-the-analyst-of-the-school-1967.pdf.

———. 2010a. Italian Note. Translated by Cormac Gallagher. *Lacan in Ireland* (blog). http://www.lacaninireland.com/web/wp-content/uploads/2010/06/Italiannote-1973.pdf.

———. 2010b. The Logic of Phantasy 1966–1967. The Seminar of Jacques Lacan, vol. XIV. Translated by Cormac Gallagher from unedited French manuscripts. Lacan in Ireland (blog), http://www.lacaninireland.com/web/

wp-content/uploads/2010/06/THE-SEMINAR-OF-JACQUES-LACAN-XIV.pdf.
———. 2011. Transference 1960–1961. The Seminar of Jacques Lacan, vol. VIII. Translated by Cormac Gallagher. Lacan in Ireland (blog). http://hdl.handle.net/10788/158.
———. 2014. *Anxiety*. The Seminar of Jacques Lacan, vol. X. Edited by Jacques-Alain Miller and translated by A. R. Price. Cambridge: Polity Press.
———. 2016. *The Sinthome 1975–1976*. The Seminar of Jacques Lacan, vol. XXIII. Edited by Jacques-Alain Miller and translated by A. R. Price. Cambridge: Polity Press.
Lévi-Strauss, Claude. 1987. *Introduction to the Work of Marcel Mauss (1950)*. Translated by Felicity Baker. London: Routledge & Kegan Paul.
Mauss, Marcel. 1923. Essai sur le don forme et raison de l'échange dans les sociétés archaïques. *L'Année sociologique (1896/1897–1924/1925)* 1: 30–186.
———. 2001. *A General Theory of Magic*. Translated by Robert Brain. London: Routledge.
McGowan, Todd. 2019. *Emancipation After Hegel*. New York: Columbia University Press.
Miller, Jacques-Alain. 1997. The Drive is Speech. *Umbr(a): On the Drive* 1: 15–33.
———. 2009. Another Lacan. *The Symptom* 10 (Spring), 1–8.
———. 2010. Extimité: extrait du cours de l'année 1985–1986: séance du 27 novembre 1985. *Letterina* 55 (56): 13–27.
Orwell, George. 2020. *The Road to Wigan Pier*. Oxford: Oxford University Press.
Rabaté, Jean-Michel. 2009. 68+ 1: Lacan's année érotique. *Parrhesia* 6: 28–45.
Ruda, Frank. 2016. *Abolishing Freedom: A Plea for a Contemporary Use of Fatalism*. Lincoln: University of Nebraska Press.
Schuster, Aaron. 2017. Impossible Professions, and How to Defend Them. In *Homestead of Dilution*, ed. Domenico Mangano, Marieke van Rooy, and Niekolaas Johannes Lekkerkerk. Eindhoven: Onomatopee.
Tupinambá, Gabriel. 2021. *The Desire of Psychoanalysis: Exercises in Lacanian Thinking*. Evanston: Northwestern University Press.
Žižek, Slavoj. 2009. *The Monstrosity of Christ: Paradox or Dialectic?* Cambridge, MA: MIT Press.
Zupančič, Alenka. 2000. *Ethics of the Real: Kant, Lacan*. London: Verso.
———. 2016. The End. *Provocations* 1: 1–19.

Index[1]

[1] Note: Page numbers followed by 'n' refer to notes.

M. Tal, *The End of Analysis*, The Palgrave Lacan Series,
https://doi.org/10.1007/978-3-031-29889-9

www.ingramcontent.com/pod-product-compliance
Lightning Source LLC
Chambersburg PA
CBHW071246180926
51613CB00002B/153
9783031298882